General Editor: Graham Handley

Brodie's Notes on Mrs Gaskell's

North and South

Graham Handley MA PhD

Formerly Principal Lecturer in English and Head of the English Department, College of All Saints, Tottenham

For Ann Allen, with love

First published 1988 by Pan Books Ltd

Reprinted 1992 by
THE MACMILLAN PRESS LTD
Houndmills, Basingstoke, Hampshire RG21 2XS
and London
Companies and representatives
throughout the world

ISBN 0-333-58097-4

Printed and bound in Great Britain by
Antony Rowe Ltd, Chippenham and Eastbourne

Contents

References in these Notes are to the Penguin Classics edition of *North and South* but as each chapter is analysed separately, the Notes may be used with any edition of the book.

Preface by the general editor

The intention throughout this study aid is to stimulate and guide, to encourage your involvement in the book, and to develop informed responses and a sure understanding of the main details.

Brodie's Notes provide a clear outline of the play or novel's plot, followed by act, scene, or chapter summaries and/or commentaries. These are designed to emphasize the most important literary and factual details. Poems, stories or non-fiction texts combine brief summary with critical commentary on individual aspects or common features of the genre being examined. Textual notes define what is difficult or obscure and emphasize literary qualities. Revision questions are set at appropriate points to test your ability to appreciate the prescribed book and to write accurately and relevantly about it.

In addition, each of these Notes includes a critical appreciation of the author's art. This covers such major elements as characterization, style, structure, setting and themes. Poems are examined technically – rhyme, rhythm, for instance. In fact, any important aspect of the prescribed work will be evaluated. The aim is to send you back to the text you are studying.

Each study aid concludes with a series of general questions which require a detailed knowledge of the book: some of these questions may invite comparison with other books, some will be suitable for coursework exercises, and some could be adapted to work you are doing on another book or books. Each study aid has been adapted to meet the needs of the current examination requirements. They provide a basic, individual and imaginative response to the work being studied, and it is hoped that they will stimulate you to acquire disciplined reading habits and critical fluency.

Graham Handley 1991

Mrs Gaskell: Life and works

Elizabeth Stevenson, later to become the novelist Mrs Gaskell, was born in Chelsea on 29 September 1810. Just over a year later her mother died, and she was brought up by her aunt Lumb in Knutsford, Cheshire, the small town Elizabeth was to immortalize as Cranford. Her father had given up the Ministry on the eve of his marriage (compare him with Mr Hale's wrestling with his conscience in *North and South*), and afterwards became Keeper of the Records at the Treasury. He was a writer of wide interests, but had little or nothing to do with the upbringing of his daughter. He remarried, while Elizabeth in distant Knutsford received the love and affection of her adoptive aunt; 'Oh there will never be one like her' she was to write much later. The first twelve years of Elizabeth's life found her coming under the influence of the Unitarians and more particularly the chapel in Brook Street which is described in some detail in Chapter 14 of *Ruth* (1853). She did, however, keep up a close relationship with her brother John; he left on a voyage to India in 1828–9 and never returned. Ironically, this provided his sister with one of the recurring motifs of her work, the lover or brother who is lost but who, in the world of fiction as distinct from life, returns – like Poor Peter in *Cranford*, Kinraid in *Sylvia's Lovers* and, appositely here, Frederick in *North and South*.

Mrs Gaskell was educated largely at the Misses Byerley's school in Warwickshire, where the discipline was firmly affectionate and, perhaps even more important, there was a systematic study of literature. Elizabeth left the school in 1827, and there is little detail on the immediately following period of her life. Her father died in March 1829, and in 1831 she met William Gaskell, a Unitarian. They were married in Knutsford in August 1832. They settled in Manchester, her home for the next thirty-three years. Her husband, a minister, lectured on a variety of subjects at Manchester New College.

In July 1833 Mrs Gaskell gave birth to a still-born child. Three years later she wrote a sonnet to the child which ends with the words

I think of thee in these far happier days,
And thou, my child, from thy bright heaven see
How well I keep my faithful vow to thee.

Her daughter Marianne was born in 1834, followed by another daughter, Meta, in 1837. She was completely engrossed in her children (though she also helped her husband with his lectures) and later wrote of the experience of motherhood:

When I had *little* children I do not think I could have written stories, because I should have become too much absorbed in my *fictitious* people to attend to my *real* ones.

She kept a detailed diary of her daughter Marianne's activities. In 1837 her beloved aunt Lumb died, leaving her a small legacy. As her husband's position improved, so Elizabeth was able to travel abroad. Her third daughter Flossy was born in 1842, and a son William in 1844. He died ten months later, and her husband urged her to write 'to turn her thoughts from the subject of her grief'. In 1846 there was some immediate compensation with the birth of her daughter Julia.

Soon her first literary efforts were published in *Howitt's Journal*, and this was followed by *Mary Barton*. The novel effectively established Mrs Gaskell as a major writer, though she had to face the criticism of those who thought that she had been guilty of giving a one-sided picture of the industrial situation. The period is the economic depression of 1839–42, the 'hungry forties', and Mrs Gaskell was quick to react to criticism, observing that 'no praise could compensate me for the self-reproach I shall feel if I have written unjustly'. She hadn't, though her novel has something of the documentary about it; her theme, explored again and again, is the preaching of kindness and reconciliation. Melodrama and realism are mixed, the realism markedly present in that terrible scene where John Barton relieves the distress of the Davenport family, and the melodrama in the story of the fallen Esther, who is too good to fall and has too much heart to be a convincing prostitute. Carlyle and Dickens were among those who admired *Mary Barton*; in May 1849 she attended a dinner given by Dickens to celebrate the publication of the first number of *David Copperfield*.

Dickens was anxious to secure Mrs Gaskell for his new journal *Household Words* (published 30 March 1850) and his first issue contained her story 'Lizzie Leigh', which dealt with prostitution. Meanwhile she and her family moved to a larger house in Plymouth Grove in 1850; later Elizabeth met Charlotte Brontë, to whom she was strongly drawn and for whom she felt great compassion. Meanwhile she continued to send stories to *Household Words*, the first sections of *Cranford* appearing in 1851. There was an early incident with Dickens;

Mrs Gaskell had made the sad Captain Brown read *Pickwick Papers*, but Dickens altered this to Hood's *Poems* without consulting the author, who was very angry. Dickens wrote 'I would do anything rather than cause you a minute's vexation', but the renewal of their partnership in the serial publication of *North and South* was to cause her many uneasy hours. As Winifred Gérin observes, Mrs Gaskell showed 'a total disregard for the basic principles of serial publication, punctuality and regulation of length.'

She drew herself voluntarily away from the light and charming humour of *Cranford* to the direct social, moral and sexual concerns of *Ruth*. Although that novel is flawed by melodramatic situations (the return of Ruth's seducer Bellingham under the name of Donne is totally improbable), *Ruth* presents the problem of the unmarried mother and the hypocrisy of self-righteously religious people who lack compassion, humility and Christian charity. The book raised an outcry. Mrs Gaskell knew what she had done, but the courage that it took to write the book is seen in the following statement in a letter to her sister-in-law:

Of course it is a prohibited book in *this*, as in many other households . . . but I have spoken out my mind in the best way I can, and I have no doubt that what was meant so correctly must do some good.

The writing and publication of *North and South* is dealt with elsewhere in this commentary, but we may note in passing Mrs Gaskell's opinion of the novel when, at the end of the serial publication, she wrote 'I meant it to have been so much better.' Her next major venture was *The Life of Charlotte Brontë* (1857), undertaken at the request of Mr Brontë, in which Mrs Gaskell set out to make the world 'honour the woman as much as they have admired the writer'. Charlotte Brontë had died of what Winifred Gérin calls 'a combination of pregnancy-sickness and the lung trouble which was the old curse taking its toll of the last member of the family.' Mrs Gaskell, with Christian forthrightness and a failure to check some of her facts, got into considerable trouble, and her publishers were threatened with a libel action if certain passages were not withdrawn from the second edition. Mrs Gaskell also had to issue a public apology to Mrs Robinson, whom she credited with ruining Branwell. When all that is allowed, the sympathetic quality of the writing and the dedication to her subject make Mrs Gaskell's biography a classic in its own right. It is full of compassionate ardour and its omissions – like the suppression of Charlotte's love for Monsieur Héger – spring from Mrs Gaskell's determination to make sure that her subject was seen in the right light.

In Rome she met Charles Eliot Norton, a student of art history, sixteen years her junior. They were strongly attracted to each other: he thought her 'like the best things in her books; full of generous and tender sympathies, of thoughtful kindness, of pleasant humour, of quick appreciation, of utmost simplicity and truthfulness . . .' The friendship was an abiding one, in no way encroaching upon her married life or her devotion to her husband and family. As she continued to write she seemed to become more aware of the art of the novel on the one hand, the possibilities of the *novella* on the other and of the need for structural coherence in her serious work. I say serious because Mrs Gaskell continued to produce work that varied remarkably in quality. Here I intend to mention only the two *novellas Lois the Witch* and *Cousin Phillis*, and the novels *Sylvia's Lovers* and *Wives and Daughters*. The first two show her masterly sense of narrative tension, her ability to control pathos and poignancy and, in relatively short compass, to probe the nature of such things as religious bias, superstition and insanity (*Lois the Witch*); the sadness of a quiet, simple and apparently returned love (*Cousin Phillis*). *Sylvia's Lovers* (1863) is very nearly a masterpiece. The story of Sylvia's love for Kinraid and, unknown to her, his being taken by the press gang, is masterly in its early execution. Even better is Sylvia's cousin Philip's concealment of Kinraid's seizure; his marriage to Sylvia; the execution of her father Daniel Robson for his part in a riot at the Randyvowse; finally, the return of Kinraid. All this is in splendid, moving, graphic narrative. Unfortunately the last section of the novel is lacking in realism and credibility. *Sylvia's Lovers* was almost four years in the writing and research, which is obvious. Unfortunately the vibrant fluency of the first part gives way to the contrived melodramatics of the final section.

Mrs Gaskell's last work, *Wives and Daughters*, was marginally incomplete at her death in 1865. It is a brilliantly evocative and ironic picture of provincial life, containing a natural and sympathetic heroine Molly Gibson; her dry and totally convincing father, a country doctor; and the latter's second wife Mrs Kirkpatrick, one of the finest and funniest portrayals in English fiction of a vain, silly and superficial egoist. *Wives and Daughters* is unflawed, and there is every indication that Mrs Gaskell had reached a high level of artistic maturity. But, having worked so hard to provide her husband with a country home in Hampshire for his retirement, she died there suddenly in November 1865. Her contribution to the development of the

English novel is no mean one. In psychological integration and consistency she comes somewhere near her great contemporary George Eliot in the presentation of her characters. She writes sometimes with a delightful and delicate wit, with historical exactitude and a sure sense of location, with searching social and moral comment and always with humanity. Sometimes the Christian message of reconciliation is overstated, yet such is her awareness that everyone is presented within the framework of compassionate irony. If she is not in the first rank of such 19th-century English novelists as Dickens, George Eliot and Hardy, she is close to it. *North and South* is relevant to our own time, since the conflicts of masters and men and their interactions are as pertinent and potent today as they were in her time. But there is a certain naiveté and goodness in Mrs Gaskell that is mainly absent from today's modes of sophisticated bargaining. The humanity of Mrs Gaskell's writing is perhaps her greatest claim to our attention.

Writing and publication of *North and South*

The novel in the form of a serial had virtually been initiated by Dickens with the publication of *Pickwick Papers* in the 1830s. Monthly publication became a common practice, and when Mrs Gaskell undertook to write *North and South* she was faced with an even greater degree of constriction, since her novel came out weekly in Dickens's magazine *Household Words*. Dickens was a great admirer of Mrs Gaskell, but there had already been a slight brush between them when he had tried to alter an emphasis in her 'The Old Nurse's Story' which had appeared in the extra Christmas number of *Household Words* for 1852. In 1853 Mrs Gaskell began her new novel, which was provisionally entitled *Margaret Hale*. She sent Dickens a plan and he was anxious to secure it for his magazine.

Narrative interest, suspense and the provision of incident were essential to the success of a serial. It seems strange to the modern reader that Dickens should have been at all critical, since Henry Lennox's proposal and Mr Hale's renunciation of his ministry are important focal points as the novel develops. Of course it is true that one has to wait some time for dramatic situations like the riot at the mill or the return of Frederick, but apparently Dickens expressed his dissatisfaction (though not overtly to Mrs Gaskell) from an early stage. Initially he told her not to worry about the divisions into the weekly parts, since he was quite prepared to suggest where the breaks should come. By May 1854 the other breaks, those between author and editor, had begun to appear; Dickens ceased to admire, as hitherto, all that she wrote. In June he referred Mr Hale's decision to leave the Church of England as 'a difficult and dangerous subject'. Later it is quite clear from his tone that he didn't consider *Margaret Hale* a good title; it soon became *North and South*, and Dickens recommended cutting some of the dialogue, instructing Mrs Gaskell to make the divisions in the next batch of manuscript that she sent. The first number of *North and South* appeared on 2 September 1854, but it is apparent that Mrs Gaskell followed her own plan and ignored the points that Dickens had made.

It was not a happy relationship. Yet Mrs Gaskell's letters show, in part at least, a happy involvement with the story. She wrote to Catherine Winkworth (11–14 October 1854) 'What do you think of a fire burning down Mr Thornton's *mills* and *house* as a *help* to failure? Then Margaret would rebuild them larger & better & need not go & live there when she's married. Tell me what you think: MH has just told the lie, & is gathering herself up after her dead faint; very meek & stunned & humble'. (*Letters*, 310). Towards the end of the same month she wrote to Emily Shaen 'I've got (with Margaret – I'm off at her now following your letter) when they've quarrelled, silently, after the lie and she knows she loves him, and he is trying not to love her, and Frederick is gone back to Spain and Mrs Hale is dead and Mr Bell has come to stay with the Hales, and Mr Thornton ought to be developing himself – and Mr Hale ought to die – and if I could get over the next piece I could swim through the London life beautifully into the sunset glory of the last scene.' (*Letters*, 321).

In the same letter (and it shows how seriously she took her art) she writes of Thornton 'I want to keep his character consistent with itself, and large, and strong, and tender, and *yet a master* . . .' But the strain of conforming to Dickens's editorial restrictions was obviously a heavy one. In December she asked him to '*keep the MS for me and shorten it as you think best for H.W.* I shall be very glad. Shortened I see it must be.' (*Letters*, 323). This surely indicates that she wanted the manuscript back so that she could work at it and expand it after the magazine publication. In the same letter just quoted she says, 'I think a better title than *North and South* would have been 'Death & Variations'. Later she sought the advice of Anna Jameson about the ending of her novel being all 'huddled and hurried up'. A few weeks before the end of the magazine issue she observed that 'I've been sick of writing, and everything connected with literature.' Finally she wrote to Dickens that 'I dare say I shall like my story, when I am a little further from it; at present I can only feel depressed about it.' (*Letters*, 323). When the serial finished publication in January 1855 Dickens was outwardly content, saying, 'Let me congratulate you on the conclusion of your story.' Later he sent her an additional £50.

The publication of the novel in volume form allowed Mrs Gaskell to make the adjustments she felt were required by her artistic integrity. Nevertheless, the prefatory paragraph to the novel, explaining this, reflects a mind conscious of being injured. Such phrases as 'obliged to conform to the conditions imposed', 'the author found it impossible to develop the story in the manner originally intended,' and, more especially, 'was compelled to hurry on events with an improbable rapidity towards the close,' indicate something akin to resentment. The result of this feeling was that three chapters were altered in the sense that they were expanded, while two new chapters were added, 'Not All a Dream' (very brief) and 'Once and Now' (the Helstone revisited chapter), numbered 45 and 46 in the Penguin edition. Certainly the Helstone chapter, though it smacks of some contrivance (the trees are felled, the cat is roasted, the parsonage has changed) is important to our understanding of how far Margaret has come in her journey towards self-realization. The treatment is basically realistic since it is Margaret's individual psychology in which we are mainly interested. The very short chapter (45) does not add greatly to the artistic effect, but Chapter 46 is full of incident, is strikingly written, its effects heightening the contrast between Margaret as she was and Margaret as she is. Helstone, one should point out, is unchanged; the changes are within Margaret. She is no longer the vicar's daughter with a kind of natural gentility; she is now a woman, and we choose the word deliberately, since it complements Thornton's use of the word 'man'. If the *Household Words* text had remained intact the effect of the novel's being abbreviated would have been correspondingly greater; it is still good to see Mrs Gaskell's sense of the novelist's responsibility in her concern to give her work balance and coherence. This is what the volume edition has achieved.

NOTE: No *Plot Summary* is given of *North and South*, since it is felt that the chapter summaries and commentaries provide the student with the sense of unravelling the novel as it first appeared in serial form, despite the author's later additions, which are incorporated.

Background

J. G. Sharps has pointed out that both *Mary Barton* (1848) and *North and South* treat the 'Condition of England Question'; this is only partly true. The same writer emphasizes that it would be a distortion to call *Mary Barton* a working-class story, though *North and South* is more obviously a middle-class romance. Yet the industrial background here is just as important as it is in the earlier novel. In 1842 there was much comment and evaluation of the poverty in Manchester (this was the period of *Mary Barton*), but by the 1850's (the time of *North and South*) the conditions of the working-classes had somewhat improved. The descriptions of the Higgins and Boucher homes have the authentic touch of the knowledgeable observer, and are relatively free from middle-class condescension. These backgrounds, and the Thornton home, mirror the treatment of the industrial and personal themes in the novel, for these themes are dependent very strongly on a sense of observed and accurate place.

Mrs Gaskell's own awareness of the problems of industrial relations – the factory system if you like – is seen in Bessy's account of how she came to contract terminal consumption through cotton fluff, by-product of the carding process. It is also seen in the views of Higgins, the reactions of Boucher, and in employers as various as Thornton and Hamper. Mrs Gaskell sees these divisions as reparable through Christian and personal influence. She sees many of the workers as biased and bloody-minded, as are their masters, and she sees the danger of extreme positions, whether it be the tyranny of the autocratic master on the one hand or the absolute power of union coercion on the other. She also records the phenomenon which still exists today, the influence of the professional opportunist or agitator on events which demand human adjustment and communion.

Chapter summaries, critical commentary, textual notes and revision questions

Chapter 1 'Haste to the Wedding'

Margaret and Edith together, with Edith fallen asleep, making preparations for the wedding. There is detail on Margaret's having stayed in Harley Street so often before; as Edith sleeps Margaret overhears the conversation between her aunt and her guests. The differences between Margaret and her cousin are indicated. Margaret goes up to the room she first came to some nine years previously. When she returns she displays Edith's shawls and dresses, and later talks to the lawyer Henry Lennox. Edith also appears proudly with Captain Lennox.

Commentary

There is a delightfully ironic tone about this opening which reminds one of Mrs Gaskell's quietly humorous observation in *Cranford*. It also provides an effective contrast with what is to come – this is the complacently indolent South, whereas most of the action of the novel (and of Margaret's experience) is to be spent in the troubled, hard and suffering North. The major technique of the novel, the seeing of everything through Margaret's consciousness, is employed at the outset. The irony plays over the spoilt Edith and her superficial life, which is immediately contrasted with the intensity of Margaret's reactions, nostalgia and basic sincerity. The dinner-party comes in for more overt ironic treatment. The treatment of marriage is shown in Mrs Shaw's reminiscences about the General and the age disparity in that marriage (compare with the marriage of Mr and Mrs Hale). Margaret's emotional nature is revealed when she thinks back to her childhood sufferings; she also shows her awareness (and some little contempt) for the triviality of the wedding preparations. There is an ease and naturalness about the dialogue, though a clear indication too of the suave and superficial personality of Henry Lennox. The ironic tone is maintained until the end of the chapter, from Mrs Shaw's ailments to Edith's spoilt showing-off her Captain. The central focus for the reader is always Margaret.

Wooed and married and a This motto, above the chapter, which mirrors
its contents, may have been written by Mrs Gaskell herself.

Corfu An Ionian island, a sometime British Protectorate but given up to
Greece in 1864.

keeping a piano in good tune . . . married life Note the Gaskellian
irony, which runs throughout this chapter.

Helstone This name was probably chosen to reflect Mrs Gaskell's
admiration of Charlotte Brontë. Caroline Helstone is one of the heroines of
Charlotte Brontë's novel *Shirley* (1849).

the mots i.e. witty remarks, sayings.

The course of true love . . . smooth *A Midsummer Night's Dream* I, 1, 134.

Belgravia Fashionable district in the West End of London.

Delhi The capital of India.

intelligence News.

with a kind of cat-like regret The striking adjective reveals Mrs Gaskell's
originality of mind. Note also the emphasis on Margaret's physicality.

Naples Port in S.W. Italy; third largest city in the country.

like the Sleeping Beauty Part of Mrs Gaskell's technique of emphasizing
the romantic nature of Edith as distinct from Margaret's sense of reality.

the mushroom rival i.e. growing suddenly, appearing overnight.

Playing with shawls . . . drawing up settlements Typical clever Henry
Lennox antithesis.

by what you call a whirlwind A phrase that is almost prophetic of the
sudden proposals of Lennox and Thornton.

with roses growing all over them The rose comes to symbolize Margaret
herself.

Tennyson's poems Mrs Gaskell was a great admirer of Tennyson – later
she uses some stanzas from *In Memoriam* as a chapter motto.

a victim to an uncongenial marriage The ironic appraisal continues
effectively. But note the contrast with Edith's forthcoming marriage,
which, since it is romantic, will, we hope, be congenial.

complaisant i.e. determined to please, obliging.

like the gipsy-encampment Another underlining of Edith's romantic
nature.

Chapter 2 Roses and Thorns

Margaret travelling home with her father and pondering on the past.
There is mention of her brother Frederick's being unable to return to
England; this is followed by a description of Margaret. Mrs Hale has
for some time found Helstone uncongenial, dwells on Frederick's
being denied to them, but has the loyal attendance of her servant
Dixon, who had tended her in her 'better' times as Miss Beresford.
Margaret is preparing to go sketching, when Henry Lennox comes on
an unexpected visit.

Commentary

The motto, nostalgic and sentimental, by Mrs Hemans, sufficiently indicates Margaret's attachment to Helstone. The comparative poverty of the Hales is stressed, and Mrs Gaskell's retrospect at the expense of Mrs Hale is laced with irony. Margaret's observation of her father shows he is subject to 'habitual distress and depression'. We notice already that Margaret, indispensable in Harley Street, will certainly be so again at home. The reference to Frederick marks his importance in the structure of the plot. In one superb paragraph, which describes Margaret walking through the woods at the end of July, we get a strong sense of her sexuality and strength; this will be needed in view of the weaknesses displayed by her parents. We note Margaret's snobbery about people in trade, her range of reading, and the delicate hints of the Hales' incompatibility. The introduction of Dixon shows Mrs Gaskell underlining the family dissonance, since Dixon is closer in some ways to Mrs Hale than is Margaret; Mr Hale too is shut out. Margaret has the perception to sense that there is something wrong, but with typical youthfulness swings back to optimism. Mrs Gaskell is adept at indicating change of mood and adept too at ending a chapter on a note of climax.

Mrs Hemans (1793–1835) The quotation in the motto is from her poem *The Spells of Home.* Mrs Hemans was very popular throughout the nineteenth century.

chip bonnet A bonnet having strips of wood, very thin, woven into the material.

the part of Figaro The reference is to Rossini's opera, written in 1816 and based on Beaumarchais's *The Barber of Seville* (1775). Figaro sings that he is in constant demand.

habitual distress and depression A hint of an inward burden, which Mr Hale is shortly to reveal to Margaret.

crushing down the fern with a cruel glee An indication of Margaret's power and sexuality.

Her mother . . . so much discontented with their situation Note the family likeness to Mrs Shaw.

I don't like shoppy people Margaret's snobbery is evident – the novel is about the education of her feelings and her views.

that she almost danced One of the few times in the novel when Margaret is really happy.

backgammon A board game for two people, which is still played today.

Thomson's Seasons, Hayley's Cowper, Middleton's Cicero The first long poem published 1726–30 by the major early 18th-century writer James Thomson (1700–48). William Hayley (1745–1820), wrote a biography of William Cowper (1731–1800). Conyers Middleton (1683–1750) wrote a *Life of Cicero* which was published in 1741.

the belles of Rutlandshire i.e. from the smallest English county, perhaps with the ironic overtone that they are small-minded people.

the good and protecting fairy . . . giant A continuation of the romance-fairy story irony. Mrs Hale can't cope with reality.

noticed an absence of mind Another hint of his secret.

arbutus i.e. of the genus Arbutus, the strawberry-tree of Southern Europe, having white or pinkish flowers, evergreen leaves and strawberry-like berries.

Chapter 3 'The More Haste the Worse Speed'

Ostensibly Henry Lennox has come to call on Margaret, bringing news of Edith. Left to himself temporarily, he takes stock of the drawing-room and estimates Mr Hale's position. Margaret meanwhile finds her mother fretful at the thought of entertaining a visitor. She takes Henry Lennox sketching; this is followed by luncheon. After that Margaret and Henry walk in the garden, and Henry proposes to her. She rejects him, is conscious of hurting him, but has to be truthful and direct in her response.

Commentary

This fine chapter shows Margaret's independence, moral courage and integrity. She is naturally well-bred, sincere in her welcome to Henry Lennox, who has come from that broader and more sophisticated life she herself has known in Harley Street. We notice immediately the inadequacy of Mrs Hale; hers is a naturally complaining nature, but there is the additional irony here that even at this stage she may well be suffering from terminal illness. The incident with the old man shows Lennox's opportunist nature, though we are told that usually he 'premeditated his actions'. Mr Hale continues to suffer silently, but the compelling sympathetic focus is on Margaret: she is completely innocent and largely unaware. This and the 'unpretending simplicity of the parsonage ways' tell on Lennox, who is moved to propose 'almost in spite of himself'. Margaret has a strong capacity for self-blame, but Lennox's coldness of tone after his rejection, and his lack of emotional tact, conspire to make her harden herself against him. Almost in reflex he shows his cynical and sarcastic nature in conversation with Mr Hale after this, though the chapter ends with his real feelings breaking through his flippancy.

This first testing of Margaret, though causing her much anguish, is the precursor of others that bring out the fineness of her character.

Mrs Browning Elizabeth Barrett (1806–61) married the poet Robert Browning after eloping with him in one of the major 19th century (factual) romances. She continued writing poetry under the name, Elizabeth Barrett Browning. The extract is from *The Lady's Yes*. Again note its appropriateness to this chapter.

'parler du soleil . . . rayons' 'Speak of the sun and one sees the sunshine' i.e. when you think or speak of someone he is certain to appear (as we might say, 'Speak of the devil').

thought Hampshire could come in i.e. that you could consider coming here.

verbenas This generally has red, white or purple fragrant flowers.

***Paradiso* of Dante** This is one of the three parts of *The Divine Comedy* by Dante Alighieri (his full name, though always called Dante), 1265–1321.

took this shape i.e. appeared like this.

in the Temple i.e. the Inns of Court, centre of the legal profession in London.

to pluck some roses . . . Symbolic here of her love for the place and for simple things.

arrière-pensée Afterthought.

cramoisy Crimson.

beurres i.e. a type of pear.

Mine be a cot beside the hill A quotation from *The Wish* by Samuel Rogers (1763–1855).

she wished herself back with her mother . . . away from him This reveals Margaret's innocence, inexperience, and also her vulnerability.

the story of the eastern king . . . lifetime Angus Easson has pointed out that the allusion is to be found in Maturin's *Melmoth the Wanderer* and in Dickens's *Hard Times* (the first chapter of the second book), which preceded *North and South* as a serial in *Household Words*.

Chapter 4 Doubts and Difficulties

Margaret experiences some natural reaction after Henry Lennox has departed, but she has to give herself first of all to the trivialities of Mrs Hale and then to the 'serious to us all' decision made by her father. He tells her that they must leave Helstone since in conscience he cannot continue to be a minister of the Church. Worse than that, he reveals that he has not yet told his wife, and they are to move within a fortnight. They are to go to Milton-Northern, a large industrial town in Darkshire. He talks of his old friend Mr Bell who owns some property there; Mr Hale intends to set up as a private tutor.

Commentary

The subtlety of Mrs Gaskell's characterization is seen here in the interaction between Margaret and her father. The latter is completely dependent on his daughter, who becomes the stay of the family. Though Mr Hale is capable of acting on what seems to be a rather vaguely defined question of principle, he is obviously a weak character. A portrait of his marriage is being drawn, with Mr Hale unable to confide fully in his ailing and complaining wife, who is certainly inadequate. The quality of the dialogue, with Margaret's limpid sincerity and Mr Hale's abject doubts and frailty, is excellently sustained. It shows Mrs Gaskell's range and her control here of a different kind of drama from that of the previous chapter. The narrative tension is maintained; we move from Margaret's personal sudden crisis with Henry Lennox to the more deeply poignant and immediate crisis of imminent change and increased emotional responsibility. Again the irony is apparent, for Margaret has built her future happiness around the ideal of the permanence of Helstone.

Habington The motto quotes lines from *Castara* (1640) by William Habington (1605–64).

He was gone Note the effective economy and finality of this opening.

giddy Flighty, unreliable.

a minister in the Church of England See Angus Easson's admirable note in the World's Classics edition of *North and South* where he points out that Mr Hale's conscience will not allow him to accept that 'the Church of England has any right to compel men's beliefs.'

the two thousand . . . from their churches A reference to St Bartholomew's Day 1662 when roughly this number, holding Church of England livings, were ejected. They could not subscribe to the Act of Uniformity which demanded complete adherence to everything contained in the Book of Common Prayer.

Mr Oldfield . . . or more (1627–82) ejected from his living in 1662. Angus Easson says that Mrs Gaskell's source for the long quotation was *The Apology of Theophilus Lindsey* (1774).

Sodom apples i.e. degraded, depraved.

Milton-Northern Manchester.

not answer i.e. would not be good enough.

Plymouth College A name conveniently to hand, since Mrs Gaskell was living at Plymouth Grove in Manchester.

What in the world . . . classics Ironically, these anticipate exactly Mrs Thornton's views, which are forcibly expressed later.

if I were but myself i.e. on my own.

Chapter 5 Decision

Margaret throws herself into her mother's parochial activities, but Mrs Hale notices that she is not looking well. Margaret prays with her father, and has a strange dream that night. The next day she breaks the news of their move to her mother. This is done piecemeal in order to lessen its effect, but Mrs Hale breaks down in remonstrance when her husband returns later. Dixon goes too far in commenting on the 'terrible news' to Margaret, who responds by putting her firmly in her place. Mrs Hale becomes ill, and Margaret goes so far as to arrange that when they move (taking Dixon with them), her mother will stay at Heston, 'a pleasant little bathing-place', while she and her father search out a suitable dwelling in Milton-Northern.

Commentary

A telling emphasis on Margaret's inward suffering as she helps her mother, realizing that everything is being done for the last time. Mrs Hale has some sensitivity, as we see when she realizes that Margaret is unwell; the church tower is used effectively to convey Margaret's changed mood. Her dream after the prayer with her father is a brilliant underlining of her fears and her insecurity. The bonnet symbolizes her in her free country life, now alas to finish; Lennox's death in her dream, his failure in that life with his proposal to her.

The switch back to the Harley Street drawing-room is an unconscious prophecy of the future; Margaret will return there when she is an heiress and, though Lennox will be alive in the flesh he will be dead to her in spirit because of her love for Thornton. Mrs Gaskell is an unerring analyst of the subconscious, as we see from the immediacy of this experience. Mr Hale's weakness is further shown when he goes out for the day in order to leave Margaret the opportunity to break the news to her mother. Again Mrs Gaskell's insight is evident in her presentation of Mrs Hale's jealousy. The divisions between north and south are clearly indicated in the comments on trade made by mother and daughter, and Dixon comes vividly alive in her objections and her scene with Margaret. The suffering of husband and wife in their separate ways rouses our compassion and our irritation, for Mrs Gaskell is presenting rounded characters, and the nature of their marriage is being subtly explored. Increased dependence on Margaret is evident throughout.

Anon For identification of the motto's author see World's Classics edition, p.438.

porringers Small dishes with handles, used for holding soup or porridge.

schismatic i.e. someone who has separated from the established church.

Church and King . . . Rump The Rump was the despised remnant of the Long Parliament that was left after 1648. This is a Cavalier toast expressive of their loyalty to the King (Charles I).

his doubts . . . no good at Oxford A telling contemporary reference, since the Oxford Movement of the nineteenth Century (roughly dated from Keble's Assize sermon in 1833) was concerned to establish High Church principles. Mr Hale could hardly subscribe to these.

She heard him linger This paragraph should be studied as a fine example of Mrs Gaskell's graphic immediacy in description. It is superbly atmospheric.

thinking of turning Dissenter This is not true, though since he 'dissents' from the Established Church it is technically accurate.

hore-hound drop A sweet made from mint, thought to be good for the chest.

fairly i.e. almost completely.

I sometimes feel . . . gave herself airs The fact is that she does, but it is one of the most endearing traits of her character.

Chapter 6 Farewell

Margaret and her family leave Helstone. She is responsible for organizing everything, and takes her last walk round the place. The next morning they set off; they pass through London (Mrs Hale even catching a glimpse – most improbably – of Henry Lennox) and stay in a hotel for the night.

Commentary

This short chapter is the link between the past life in the South at Helstone and the new life to come in the North. The motto at the head of the chapter is most important. It is from Tennyson's *In Memoriam* (1850) that long expression of love, faith, doubt and loss in which he immortalized his own love for his friend Arthur Hallam. It was Mrs Gaskell's favourite poem, and at her funeral service the minister read some lines from it. Here it is expressive of Margaret's grief for the loss of her beloved South.

Mrs Gaskell conveys well the atmosphere of the move, including the servants' idea that because Margaret is controlled she cannot care much for Helstone. The strength and the suffering inherent in

Margaret's character are seen in her sentimental walk, her recollections of Henry Lennox, her passing affinity for the poachers and their freedom. When she goes indoors again she has to cope with a father who appears to be more depressed than she is. The pathos of Susan's watching for Margaret does not undermine her strength. She needs it all to deal with a father who is intent on self-pity and full of guilt for what he has done and its effect on his nearest and dearest. Her mother's fleeting glimpse of Henry Lennox, with its deliberately symbolic reminder of a bright day at Helstone, is a loose stitch in the fabric of Mrs Gaskell's narrative.

the Temple Gardens See note p.20.
Camilla a fast-moving princess of the Volsces referred to in Virgil's *Aeneid*, Book 8.
the last drop i.e. the final depressing fact.
they sat with him on the ground See Job, 2,13.

Chapter 7 New Scenes and Faces

Heston described, and then Margaret and Mr Hale house-hunt in Milton-Northern. They are full of criticism of what they see, Margaret in particular. Mr Thornton calls to see them. Margaret sees him – her father is out visiting a house – and there is a full description of her and of the impression she makes on her visitor. With Mr Hale's return there is talk of Mr Bell. After Thornton leaves he instructs the landlord of the house they are taking to make the alterations they require. Meanwhile Mr Hale and Margaret tell Mrs Hale about Thornton.

Commentary

The chapter is dominated by the description of the meeting between Margaret and Thornton. The latter obviously resents what he observes as her haughty and superior manner and she, with her southern snobbery, tends anyway to look down on someone in trade. Before that there is the effect on father and daughter of the crowded industrial streets, and Margaret reveals here her practical ability to plan their new lives within these new and crowded constraints. The simple power of Margaret's personality is evident when she speaks to Thornton; but he is magnetized by her beauty and sexual attraction – superbly conveyed by Mrs Gaskell in such phrases as 'full of a soft feminine defiance' and 'her round white flexile throat rising out of the full, yet lithe figure'. Other words like 'cold' and 'proud indifference' are also used, but we who have come to know Margaret realize that she has a cover for her feelings anyway.

There is a superb sense of contrast and conflict between Margaret and Thornton but even here there is a subtle irony. Margaret appears to have the supposed coldness of the North and Thornton the supposed passion of the South. This perhaps anticipates their coming blend, the consummation that each will ultimately find in the other. In retailing their news to her mother, Margaret further reveals her own snobbery.

Matthew Arnold (1822–88) The poem in the motto was written in 1849, and the third line shows Mrs Gaskell's memory to be faulty – it should read 'Hem me round everywhere'.

smock-frocks Loose protective overgarments worn by farm labourers.

hopeless streets A fine choice of adjective – there is no hope in this poverty, monotony, sameness.

unparliamentary smoke As laid down by the Town Improvement Causes Act of 1847 any new fireplace or furnace had to eliminate smoke from the atmosphere by consuming it as it arose. The Act was ineffectual and was easily abused.

as an empress wears her drapery This kind of image conveys the inherent, simple nobility of Margaret's character.

flexile Pliable; a variant of the more common 'flexible'.

niche i.e. role in life.

sagacious, and strong, as becomes a great tradesman Margaret is, I think, being ironic.

Chapter 8 Home Sickness

The description of their early suffering in Milton, with an emphasis on the fogs; there is the contrast of a letter from Edith, and Margaret is moved to reminisce about Harley Street; also to think of what might have been between herself and Henry Lennox. Mrs Hale becomes ill, Mr Hale gains some pupils, foremost among them Mr Thornton, while Dixon becomes more crotchety and Margaret tries to get a servant to help her with the work. Margaret and her father often take walks, and one day she meets a man and a girl with whom she has struck up a kind of friendship. She gives the girl some flowers; the girl is obviously very ill, and looks forward to Margaret's keeping her promise to visit them.

Commentary

The atmosphere of depression, the complementary nature of weather, place and health is well captured. Margaret indulges herself with memories of Helstone – it is her one luxury – and Edith's letter from the other South is used as a deliberate contrast. Mrs Gaskell is keeping her title well in mind, and we note the totally selfish indulgence of Edith. Margaret always has the spirit to swing back from depression, and this is well in evidence when she has overcome the might-have-been with Henry Lennox. The commercial focus on life in Milton-Northern is given a considered stress. Mr Thornton's unusual qualities are seen in his wishing to learn the classics; Mrs Hale's selfishness and emotional limitation in her jealousy of the friendship between her husband and Thornton. The contrast between north and south in terms of Mr Hale's status and the servant problem is also dwelt upon. Most important of all we notice Margaret's adjustment to their changed circumstances, with her response to the loud girls, her simple kindliness of nature and, above all, her warmth to Bessie and to Higgins, important to the plot and to the education of her own feelings.

And it's hame . . . wad I be This motto is identified by Angus Easson as being by Allan Cunningham (1784–1842).

yellow November fogs . . . circumstance This idea of using factual fog and an image of emotional and mental fog seems to derive from Dickens's *Bleak House* (1852–3), which opens with an impressive and imaginative fog description, which then gives way to a wholesale investigation of the fog of the law.

sucking situations i.e. not requiring experience, the sons are not yet 'weaned', capable of fending for themselves.

cutting away all off-shoots . . . the plant Mrs Gaskell here uses natural imagery ironically in order to mock rigid commercial practice.

Aristides . . . the Just The Athenian statesman who was surnamed the Just (see Plutarch's *Life of Aristides*) found when he met a voter that his surname had caused offence.

Louis the fourteenth (1638–1715), called the Sun King, hence the reference here. He was of course King of France.

fired up against Was angry with.

hoo Her.

country Area.

in a waste i.e. tuberculosis, the lung disease that was the scourge of the nineteenth century and the early part of this.

amaranths Fabulous flowers, the symbol of eternal life because unlike ordinary flowers they do not fade.

Whatten Why are?
set up i.e. upset.

Chapter 9 Dressing for Tea

Margaret finds that her father has invited Mr Thornton to tea on a day when she had wished to follow her own pursuits. As a result of her frustration she gets a very bad headache, but does the ironing; meanwhile, Thornton and his mother discuss the visit, Mrs Thornton fearing that Margaret is setting her cap at her son.

Commentary

In this chapter Mrs Gaskell employs her usual device of contrast. The dialogue in the Hale household reflects their coming down in the world, with Mrs Hale querulous, Margaret overworked, and Mr Hale, as ever, anxious. The snobbery of the women is evident. The contrast with the Thornton home is immediate. Thornton has obviously fallen in love with Margaret, though he would not admit it either to himself or to his mother. She, however, is not only obdurate and strong but perceptive, and sees that her son is drawn towards Margaret. Note the direct and outspoken nature of her language, even at the end of the chapter an expression of hate. The contrast between the mothers is, symbolically, that between the tough and uncompromising north and the soft and snobbish south.

Mrs Barbauld (1743–1825). The motto is a quotation from *The Groans of the Tankard*.
ad libitum According to pleasure.
Pythias to your Damon Faithful friends unto death in classical mythology, one offering himself as hostage for the other.
Matthew Henry's Bible Commentaries The author (1662–1714) of a five-volume work on the Old and New Testaments (1708–10).
a morceau de salon A fashionable piece of music (?).

Chapter 10 Wrought Iron and Gold

With Thornton's visit there is a description of the Hales' room. Margaret's movements, and particularly her bracelet, fascinate Thornton; when Margaret has the leisure to study her father and Thornton in conversation she finds herself admiring certain facets of the manufacturer. He himself is absorbed in explaining 'the might of the steam-hammer' to Mr Hale.

There follows an argument about North and South, with a stress on the dirt to be found in Milton. Thornton gives what amounts to something of a lecture on the rise of trade and the battle between masters and men. Thornton praises the rise of working men to positions of power in industry. This leads him, without conceit, to tell them of his own struggles; he feels rebuffed at his leaving when Margaret bows to him rather than shaking hands, though she is sorry that she hasn't shaken hands when she sees his intention.

Commentary

The focus is on the interaction of Margaret and Thornton. There is much sexual awareness, the emphasis on the bracelet being particularly suggestive, while the appraisal of the Hales's room by Thornton points up his awareness of the difference between them. Although Margaret's independence is evident – she hands Thornton his cup of tea 'with the proud air of an unwilling slave' – she gets over (in part) her headache sufficiently to observe the differences between her father and Thornton (the faces symbolize South and North) and feels some attraction to Thornton. Mrs Gaskell writes subtly, for though there is no overt sexual suggestion, we feel that Margaret, unknown to herself, is responding to the compulsive masculinity of the man. She becomes warm as a partisan of the South, but she listens to Thornton's exposition and learns the more because of it; this ability to listen and learn is one of Margaret's major attributes. Thornton's account of his own struggles is a moving one – again we are aware of the contrast and the comparison between the economic circumstances of Thornton and the Hales. There is no conceit in his story; we do, however, note his pride, which is not dissimilar to Margaret's.

George Herbert (1593–1633) English metaphysical poet. The motto is from his *Affliction*.
davenport A small writing desk with drawers.
until it tightened her soft flesh Strongly sexual suggestion.
'I've a hundred captains . . . was he' A traditional ballad.
that rude model of Sir Richard Arkwright's Arkwright (1732–92) was the virtual founder of the modern cotton industry through his development of the powered spinning frame in the late 1760s.
Homer The Greek epic poet, author of *The Iliad* and *The Odyssey*.
nothing like leather i.e. well-bound books and what they contain.

Revision questions on Chapters 1–10

1 Does the opening chapter in Harley Street capture your interest? Give reasons for your answer.

2 Write a detailed account of Margaret's character as it appears in these chapters.

3 Compare and contrast the three settings Mrs Gaskell uses in these chapters.

4 'Mr Hale's decision to leave the Ministry is too vague to be convincing.' Discuss.

5 Write on any aspect of the novel so far which interests you but is not covered by the questions above.

Chapter 11 First Impressions

Margaret reveals what she liked in Mr Thornton's account; Mr Hale fills in further details about it; Margaret shows her continuing snobbery by referring to Thornton's position as 'tainted' by his being a manufacturer. Later Margaret, concerned about her mother's health, finds her praying for 'patience to endure bodily suffering'. She follows this with her overdue visit to the Higginses, where Bessy's suffering is more acute than her mother's, and where Higgins's words make Margaret feel guilty for her omission. Bessy has got religion; she also has a great love for her father. Margaret treats her tenderly, putting Bessy's head to rest on her bosom. When she gets home she learns that Mrs Thornton and her son are to visit the Hales the next day.

Commentary

This chapter is important for its plot emphasis and for the expansion of Margaret out into the working-class area of Milton. There is more than a hint of Mrs Hale's coming terminal illness, and the social contrast, with Thornton and her own conditions, is seen in Margaret's visit to Bessy and her father. That visit symbolizes Margaret's essential goodness (despite her pride) and the beginning of her social education, which runs parallel with her own emotional development. The interaction with Higgins is interesting because of the conflict between father and daughter that covers their deep love for each other. It forms in the structural balance a neat contrast with Margaret's own domestic position. And the illness in each is, I think, a reflection of the social illness in society.

Anon The motto is unidentified. Notice its appropriateness to the character of Thornton.
the land o' Beulah See Isaiah, 62,4. The land of Israel.
getten Have got.
again Against.
took a mind to ye Liked you.
'They shall hunger no more . . .' Isaiah, 49,10.
methodee fancies Methodist ideas.
moped (Dialect) made imbecilic, silly.

Chapter 12 Morning Calls

Despite his mother's resistance, Mr Thornton persuades her to pay a visit to the Hales. We learn of Mrs Thornton's contempt for her weak daughter Fanny, who is ordered to accompany her mother on the visit despite her indolence and her affectation of illness. She reveals to Margaret her longing to go to London, and her mother's being set against it. They talk about factories, and Fanny shares Mrs Hale's antipathy to dust and dirt.

Commentary

There is further concentration on the strength and character of Mrs Thornton – hers is a spare, nothing-wasted life, and she has no time for superficiality. Like Margaret, she has a secret cross to bear – in the person of Fanny, who is all that she doesn't wish her to be. We notice her laziness and we also notice Thornton's assertiveness. Beneath all this is Mrs Thornton's possessiveness over her son, and her jealousy of Margaret. There is some fine irony about the verbal exchanges between those unlikely social mixers, the Thorntons and the Hales, bound to utter 'all the stereotyped commonplaces that most people can find to say with their senses blindfolded'. Typically, Mrs Hale responds to Mrs Thornton's lace rather than to the person who is wearing it. Fanny reveals how essentially superficial and shallow she is. The North–South divisions are further emphasized, though Margaret's recognition of what Fanny's interests should be are an indication of her own capacity.

Friends in council The source of this chapter's motto, *Essays on a variety of subjects* by Sir Arthur Helps (1813–75).

killed off i.e. paid all the necessary visits.

a burden to a song Chorus or refrain.

stereotyped commonplaces . . . blind folded Note the irony and Mrs Gaskell's scorn of this manner of speaking.

Fifteen shillings a week Margaret is thinking of Thornton's reference to his family's early struggles: 75 pence, but worth much more then.

the Tales of the Alhambra These were written by the American Washington Irving (1783–1859) and published in 1832. The Alhambra is the Moorish Palace in Spain, and Mrs Gaskell is again being ironic at the expense of romantic notions.

Chapter 13 A Soft Breeze in a Sultry Place

Margaret, once they have left, races to call on Bessy Higgins. She tells Bessy, at the latter's request, all about her home, and Bessy restlessly speaks of her wish for heaven. She also confides in Margaret her fears for her father and her love for her dead mother. She tells Margaret how she longs for death to escape from the fluff filling her lungs. There is a detailed account of this. Margaret realizes that she and Bessy are the same age. Margaret says that she will take care of Bessy's sister Mary. A year has passed since Edith's marriage. Margaret tells her father that she fears her mother is ill, but he does not accept this.

Commentary

We admire Margaret's spirit and common Christianity in visiting Bessy. The account of the fluff further underlines the divisions between masters and men, and the contrast between Margaret's lot in life and Bessy's is stressed. There is a terrible poignancy in Bessy's longing for heaven because of the sufferings she has had to endure upon earth. Margaret is learning more and more, and the passing of the year indicates the changed nature of her experiences. Mr Hale's blindness with regard to his wife is evident, though perhaps there is some subtlety here too – he simply will not see what he does not wish to see.

R. C. Trench (1807–86). The motto is from his poem *The Kingdom of God*.

rough-stoning Scouring, often employing sand to clear the dirt.

squab Defined immediately afterwards as a short sofa.

set me up Prepare me for.

dree place (Dialect) miserable place.
a carding-room The place for combing out the cotton in order to get rid of seeds. Bessy is describing what was later called card-room asthma.
gradely (Dialect) good-looking.
na Not.
nesh (Dialect) soft, weak.
come In.
your mother was so simple and open A good example of the way Mr Hale believes only what he wants to believe.
racooning Racoons are mammals that inhabit North and Central America and the West Indies, and presumably they are restless. (Spelt 'raccoon' in USA.)

Chapter 14 The Mutiny

Mrs Hale in her suffering comes back to the subject of Frederick and decides to confide in Margaret; or rather, Margaret, who wishes to know everything, persuades her to do so. Mrs Hale refers to Frederick's letters, and the process of the mutiny is described. There is some hint of Frederick's passionate nature, and Mrs Hale describes her own and her husband's reactions to the news. Obviously Mr Hale was the more broken of the two at the time, largely because of the extreme language used in the newspaper reports to describe Frederick. He will be hanged if he returns to England.

Commentary

There is something contrived about this chapter, with its retrospective treatment of the conditioning which has helped to enfeeble Mr and Mrs Hale in their separate ways. Mrs Gaskell lost a brother who never returned from a voyage, and the fictional Frederick is her imaginative treatment of the situation. There is a graphic immediacy about the description of the incident which led to the mutiny, but it is romance rather than realism that Mrs Gaskell is writing here. We recognize, however, the psychological truth in Mr Hale's breakdown and the abject behaviour of his wife, from whom at the time of crisis he had no support. The end of the chapter is masterly, with Mrs Hale shut away in her own grief, selfishly to the exclusion of Margaret, who has been trying to comfort her.

Southey (1774–1843). The motto is quoted from *The Sailor's Mother*.
Cadiz The port in S.W. Spain, originally a trading centre of the Phoenicians.

Orion Named after either the giant of that name in Greek mythology, or the constellation.

to keep slavers off i.e. those who were capturing slaves for sale.

Captain Reid was sent adrift The whole episode is reminiscent of the mutiny of the Bounty and the setting adrift of Captain Bligh.

hung at the yard-arm The traditional punishment for those found guilty at a naval court-martial.

Chapter 15 Masters and Men

Mr Hale and Margaret visit the Thorntons, and there is some detailed description of their house, the room in which they sit being a place where 'Everything reflected light, nothing absorbed it.' Margaret tells Mrs Thornton of her mother's indisposition, but Mrs Thornton pays it scant attention. She expresses some contempt for the classics, and asserts her pride in her son's role as a manufacturer. Margaret admits that she admires him, but she and Mrs Thornton are soon at cross-purposes because the mother suspects that Margaret has designs on her son. She also tells Margaret that there will probably be a strike. That evening Thornton calls on the Hales, bringing Dr Donaldson's address. Margaret and Thornton argue about class differences. Thornton stresses the need for despotism during the time he is in contact with his workpeople. Margaret's views are best put in her own words that 'God has made us so that we must be mutually dependent.'

Commentary

The chapter is virtually divided into two parts, consisting of the interaction between Margaret and Mrs Thornton and followed by that between Margaret and her son. Mr Hale's anxiety surfaces before the visit to the Thorntons. The description of the Thornton house and rooms – and the dependence of both on the factory – emphasize the differences between north and south that are going to be particularized in the characters and their conversations in this chapter. Mrs Thornton's room is her character – 'icy, snowy discomfort' – and her prejudices are strong ones. She cannot stand any fine-ladyisms, but is honest enough to respect Margaret's own honesty of utterance. Her jealousy manifests itself in her crediting (or discrediting) Margaret with having designs upon her son. Mrs Thornton gives Margaret an example of her own courage in strike-and-violence adversity, the irony being that Margaret is to display a like courage of a more intensely personal character in a similar and now imminent situation. The debate on the mutual difference of position between Margaret and Thornton is important in the structure of the novel, since both are to shift their positions somewhat despite the divisions here. This symbolizes perhaps the move towards mutual recognition and tolerance. The chapter closes exactly as an earlier one, with Margaret withholding her hand. It is a subtle indication of her fear of contact with Thornton because of her own suceptibility.

W. S. Landor (1775–1864), the motto is one of his epigrams.
lurries i.e. lorries.
'the pride that apes humility' Angus Easson gives the source as either Coleridge or Southey.
whose own crow is the whitest ever seen Probably a version of 'all her geese are swans'.
line and letter i.e. complete explanations.
tried and dodge i.e. experimented.
hedge-lawyers i.e. people always ready to argue a point.
Utopia Any real or imaginary place, state etc. which is considered to be perfect, from Sir Thomas More's book of that name published in 1516.
Plato's Republic Plato (?427–?347) BC Greek philosopher influenced by his teacher Socrates, the *Republic* being one of his most important works.
bated i.e. held back.
Nuremberg Famous city in Bavaria, SW Germany.
God ... mutually dependent Margaret is somewhat naive, but the statement is a fair assessment of capital/labour relations.
that spirit which suffereth long ... See 1 Corinthians 13:4–5 for this moving exposition of Charity.
Cromwell Oliver (1599–1658) English general, statesman and ruler.

Chapter 16 The Shadow of Death

Dr Donaldson calls, and finds Mrs Hale terminally ill. He tells Margaret the truth at her own insistence, though Mrs Hale has had the consideration to tell him not to. Donaldson is very impressed with Margaret – he is himself a bachelor – and when he has gone Margaret breaks down, recovers, and goes to see her mother. The latter really only wants to see Frederick. Dixon also breaks down, but she is reconciled to Margaret. She, Dixon, has carried the burden of the secret for some time. When Margaret has gone out Dixon admits how much she loves her.

Commentary

Margaret is her mother's daughter in one sense, and that is in her passionate jealousy, here seen with regard to Dixon and the latter's being her mother's confidante. The scene between Donaldson and Margaret is finely handled, perhaps because Donaldson, old bachelor that he is, is susceptible not only to Margaret's courage but to her physical presence and appeal. Margaret's reactions show her giving way to, then fighting this weakness, and in the background continually is the weakness of her father who, sooner or later, is going to have to face up to the situation. With typical and searing honesty she tells her mother that she has been told. Mrs Hale's hysteria in her anguish for Frederick comes after exclamations that do not ring true – 'Little first-born child, come to me once again!' The scene between Margaret and Dixon more than compensates for this, with Margaret showing true humility and Dixon true feeling. Dixon has the practical ability to get Margaret out of the house, knowing that a walk in the fresh air is the best preparation for Margaret's having to face her father.

the Elder Brother See Luke, 15.
game to the backbone Slang for 'courageous'.
Little first-born child Even Mrs Hale would not be guilty of such bathos. This is poor writing.
racked the tenants i.e. got everything out of them that he could.
ha' made a deal more on her i.e. treated her much better.
minded missus Paid more attention to his wife.

Chapter 17 What is a Strike?

Margaret, walking in the streets, notices that there are many men lounging about. She goes to the Higginses, and finds father and daughter divided over the question of the strike. Nicholas looks down on what he considers the spiritless workers of the south, who don't strike. Nicholas explains the reasons for the strike. He also gives Margaret some account of the character of Thornton as the men see him. When he goes outside to smoke his pipe Bessy tells Margaret how much men like her father have to put up with. Margaret tells Bessy that her mother is very ill, just as they were on the point of quarrelling. Bessy ponders on Margaret's goodness and the good her visit has done her.

Commentary

In some ways this approximates to the 'Masters and Men' chapter (15) in which Thornton spells out the case for the employers. This is the obverse side of the coin, with Higgins putting the case for the men and the belief that they are being exploited by the masters. But easily the most important aspect of this chapter is the fact that Margaret is taken out of herself by visiting the Higginses: it is part of her education to learn to give herself more widely and deeply despite increasing emotional demands at home. This is the index to Margaret's moral development. The contrast between north and south is maintained, though rather tenuously, through Margaret's knowledge. There is a terrible reference to children not being of factory age, and therefore not able to bring money into the family pool. Bessy is prophetic about what is going to be the result of the strike, and Nicholas shows his own obduracy at the same time as he shows his deep concern for his daughter. An interesting plot device has Margaret in her own suffering confiding in Bessy about Frederick.

Anon The motto here is identified by Angus Easson as by A. L. Waring.
welly clemmed (Dialect) almost starved.
dazed Benumbed.
again Against.
Dun yo' Don't you.
m'appen Perhaps.
none on 'em factory age By the Factory Act of 1833 it was prohibited to employ children under 9 years of age in the textile industry.
bated Lowered, reduced.
bug-a-boo Goblin.
brass (Dialect) money.
look to it i.e. watch out!
as dour as a doornail i.e. tough and strong, unyielding.
knobsticks i.e. those who work despite the fact that a strike has been called.
farred (Dialect) Out of mind.
not to say Not really.
four-pounder i.e. a large loaf weighing four pounds.
to common on i.e. to make a meal from.
to knock a man down i.e. to make him feel depressed.
And the name of the star is called Wormwood See Revelations, 8,11.
deaved (Dialect) stunned.
fustian-cutting Cutting the thread on the surface.
the like The same.

Chapter 18 Likes and Dislikes

Margaret lies to her father about the real state of her mother's health. There is also a letter from Aunt Shaw; then an invitation from Mrs Thornton to dinner. Mrs Thornton and Fanny debate the Hales – Mrs Thornton is puzzled by Margaret, but says that she doesn't think of her often. Mr Thornton reveals his belief that Margaret would not accept him if he proposed to her. He changes the subject to that of the strike, and says that he intends to get hands from Ireland if they are needed. He is disgusted by the attitude of some of his fellow employers, but is determined on his own course of action.

Commentary

Margaret manages her lie well, unlike the one she has to tell later in order to protect Frederick. In a sense, as I have indicated, Mr Hale does not want to know the truth anyway. Notice how far astray Aunt Shaw's thoughts are – and how dissonant in this context – while Margaret concentrates on giving her father the comfort she knows he craves. The debate in the Thornton family shows Fanny at her shallow worst, Mrs Thornton still jealous and protective over her son, and that son restless because of the strike situation and vulnerable to all talk of Margaret. We notice that Thornton is easily hurt by his mother's words. There is a needful filling in of the historical background, and the end of the chapter is a study in Thornton's constraint and restlessness.

Wallenstein The motto is a quote from the play by Schiller (1759–1805), German playwright, critic and poet.

Sorrento The port in S.W. Italy, a popular resort.

set her up Establish her.

rouge you up i.e. put some (natural) colour in your cheeks.

a neighbouring Lyceum i.e. lecture hall, from the name of the place in Athens where Aristotle taught.

Jezebel See particularly I Kings, 16,31; 19 and other references to the unscrupulous wife of Ahab.

told me out i.e. said it yourself.

actually turned out i.e. gone on strike.

naughts i.e. nobodies.

turn-out Strike.

go alike on tramp i.e. try to find work elsewhere.

the old combination-laws These were the laws of 1799–1800 which banned men from joining together in unions for self-protection against untrained men being employed. They were repealed in 1824.

Chapter 19 Angel Visits

There is discussion as to what Margaret should wear at the Thornton dinner-party. She tells Bessy Higgins of the engagement, and has the social divisions emphasized for her as a result. Bessy shows her interest in having Margaret appear to advantage at the party. There is the news of Higgins and 'all Hamper's men' turning out on strike, and Bessy, herself ill, tells Margaret how many of the women say that their children are starving. Higgins learns of Margaret's coming visit to Thornton's, and is in boastful vein about the strike. Margaret begins to be aware of the division in Thornton between the private and the public man, the first full of compassion for her mother and the second against the needs of the working men and their suffering which is put to him by Mr Hale. Boucher is obviously a potential strike-breaker because of the state of his family and his wife's illness in particular, but Nicholas gives him money.

Commentary

Contrast is again evident, with the dinner-party gradually being pushed into the background by the obvious growing discontent. The warmth of the friendship between Bessy and Margaret, and Bessy's free acknowledgement of what Margaret has done for her, show that human contact can transcend class and social divisions. Nicholas's arrogance gives way to Boucher's immediate need. It is obvious too that John Thornton is an obstinate man, and even his feelings for Margaret will not make him move at this stage from an entrenched and enclosed position.

Henry Vaughan The author of the motto (1622–95), late Metaphysical and mystical poet. Quoted from *Silex Scintillans* (1650).
th' first folk i.e. the best, most socially prominent people.
support the honour i.e. do justice to, easily bear (ironic here).
sevenpence a yard i.e. cheap (about 3p by today's prices).
dree See note p.32.
pre-elected i.e. destined for.
moil Work.
and the very dogs are not pitiful See Luke, 16,20.
deaved See note p.36.
plaining i.e. complaining.
in course Of course, naturally.
th' great battle of Armageddon See Revelations 16,16.
a bumper A toast.

pottered (Dialect) confused.
the five-per-cent i.e. the amount of the rise.
bout Without.
the power of the wild bird i.e. the pelican.
exoteric i.e. intended for more than a select minority.
squab See note p.31.
a'this'n Like this.
Five shilling 25 pence, but worth much more then.
welly (Dialect) almost.
sennight Week.
fou' Foul.
Hou'd Bear (up), be brave
Clem Starve.
just as good as Solomon Tenth century BC son of David and Bathsheba
 who was credited with great wisdom.
to see after i.e. take care of.
cotched (Dialect) caught.
been pulled down i.e. the situation has got him down.
cranky (Dialect) sick, ill.
a swounding daze i.e. fainting from feebleness.

Chapter 20 Men and Gentlemen

Margaret herself experiences conflict about the dinner-party because
of the sufferings of others, and this upsets the easily-distressed Mrs
Hale. Mr Hale as ever compromises when asked his opinion, but does
try to get an Infirmary Order for Mrs Boucher. Margaret dresses for
the party, and Dixon takes some delight in showing her off to Mrs
Hale. Mrs Thornton meanwhile provides lavishly, almost ostentatiously for her guests. Mr Hale queries their living so close to the
factory, but it is obvious that Mrs Thornton takes a great delight in it.
Thornton is once more struck with Margaret's beauty, and observes
her constantly while the guests assemble. Margaret in her turn
watches Thornton. She is impressed by his personality and the
obvious respect in which he is held. There is some conversation
between Thornton and Margaret about the use of the term 'gentleman'. He is called away in the middle of their discussion, and
Margaret, unknown to herself, is a focus of attention for some of the
men in the company.

Commentary

Margaret's feelings are now ever in the process of being educated, and we notice that in this chapter she and Thornton move closer together despite his preoccupation with the strike and Margaret's many worries. Mr Hale shows his ready compassion, but we can't help but feel that he is ineffectual. Mrs Thornton's lavish hospitality is at variance with her normal character, though her son delights in it and sees that it is right despite his own economic embarrassments. The set-piece descriptions of Thornton and Margaret are imbued with Mrs Gaskell's direct expression of sexuality; the emphasis on the definition of the word 'gentleman' shows their different backgrounds but their movement towards a kind of truth. There is a fine play of observation on the guests and the movement of their conversation. Thornton emerges as a very impressive individual, and Margaret's awareness of this is shown for the first time in public.

Rollo, Duke of Normandy The source of the motto is this Jacobean play, probably produced about 1616, written by Fletcher and others.

an Infirmary order i.e. a declaration saying that she couldn't afford treatment, in order to get her free treatment.

toilettes Preparations – washing, dressing etc. – before going out.

the used-up style ... old London parties i.e. artificial and superficial conversation. This aspect of the South compares unfavourably with the North.

Robinson Crusoe The novel, by Daniel Defoe, was published in 1719.

a saint in Patmos See Revelations, 1,9.

catechising i.e. questioning and testing.

Revision questions on Chapters 11–20

1 Write a character study of Mr Thornton as he appears in the novel so far.

2 Examine Mrs Gaskell's use of retrospect. How does this affect Margaret?

3 Write an account of the Higgins family, referring to information in these chapters.

4 Bring out the differences between masters and men.

5 Compare and contrast the attitude towards the illnesses of Bessy and Mrs Hale.

Chapter 21 The Dark Night

Margaret and her father walk home discussing Mr Thornton and the impending strike. They arrive home to the crisis of Mrs Hale's near death. Mr Hale collapses, shaking all over, and soon has to have the doctor's attention himself. When he comes round he accuses Margaret of being cruel in not telling him before of the true state of Mrs Hale's health. Margaret and Dixon sit up with Mrs Hale, and Margaret feels then that 'the terrible night were unreal as a dream'. Margaret walks through the crowds on an August afternoon to get a water-bed from the Thorntons. But when she gets to the factory she hears no machinery; in the distance, though, she hears the roar of a gathering crowd.

Commentary

This is a superbly managed brief chapter, with the conversation preceding the crisis heightening the dramatic effect of what is to come. As we might expect, Mr Hale proves unequal to the strain, while Margaret and Dixon each in her separate way shares the burden. As Margaret walks and thinks, and above all, feels, her inner tumult is balanced by the outer tumult that is beginning to arise. Mrs Gaskell gives this whole chapter a tremendous microcosmic relevance, the crisis of the individual mirroring the crisis of the mass. Margaret's consciousness is fully probed throughout the chapter. We note that her pride and her coldness are now in abeyance.

Elliott The motto comes from Ebenezer Elliott (1781–1849), the famous Corn Law rhymer.

Leezie Lindsay's Another reference to a traditional ballad

a bell continually tolling Prophetic of the funeral bell which will soon toll for Mrs Hale; then for her husband.

water-bed i.e. a mattress made comfortable and soft by being partly filled with water.

tempest . . . slow-surging wave . . . threatening crest A powerful pattern of imagery to convey atmosphere.

Chapter 22 A Blow and its Consequences

Margaret goes to the drawing-room and is told by Fanny the state of things, with the Irish work-force trapped in an upper mill-room. Mrs Thornton then realizes that the strikers are at the work-gates, which quiver 'like reeds before the wind'. Fanny becomes hysterical, Thornton appears, shuts the factory door, and the mob howl at him. He tries to get his mother and Margaret to move into the back rooms, and reveals that the soldiers have been sent for. Margaret sees the livid face of Boucher, and afterwards begs Thornton to go down and treat the raging men as human beings. He faces them; she watches the fierce interaction between him and the crowd, and feels that at any instant there will be an explosion. She goes down herself; urges them to disperse; the first clog is thrown; Margaret is hit by a stone and held by Thornton. The crowd moves towards the gate; Thornton supports Margaret; she half faints and Thornton, worried that she is badly injured, utters his love for her. Thornton deals with his Irish workers while Mrs Thornton attends to Margaret. Later the servant Jane reports to Fanny that Margaret had her arms round Thornton's neck. She has plaster put on her wounds by the doctor, but she has heard what the servant has said and is deeply upset and humiliated at the thought that she should be considered as having behaved forwardly with Mr Thornton.

Commentary

This is one of the finest and most graphic chapters in the novel, full of incident, fine crowd scenes and poignant, moving, passionate revelation. The immediate effects are frightening enough, Mrs Gaskell conveying the eruptive atmosphere with directness and economy. Fanny's hysteria is balanced by her brother's courage. There is a vivid inside–outside effect to begin with, with both Margaret and Mrs Thornton frightened but drawing on their reserves of courage. Margaret transcends the immediacy by her sympathetic identification with those who are suffering. Her heart is with the imported Irish workers who are likely to be the principal sufferers in any riot. The tension is conveyed by quick statement – the imminent arrival of the soldiers – and graphic description of the mob, particularized by the livid Boucher but animalized by a number of related images. Thornton is in command, and Margaret is greatly humanized, not by being in command but by being susceptible, even conscious perhaps of being wrong. The confrontation of master and men is imbued with all the dangers of extreme and irrational violence, while Margaret's action is made the more real because her voice dies away and picks up with her fear and her passionate sympathy.

When she is hit it appears to be the climax of the action; but not so, for there is the opportunist irony of the voice which tells Thornton that he has sheltered behind a woman. The drip of blood from Margaret's wound has the accompaniment of the rhythmic marching feet. Thornton's expression of love is sexually passionate, though the language is the extreme language of romance. We may allow, however, that this is an extreme moment, situation, by any standards. Mrs Thornton's determined practicality on Margaret's behalf is the measure of the woman, and is seen in contradistinction to Jane's gossip for Fanny's ears which makes Margaret ashamed when she understands the purport of it. It gives her the strength to leave; but in a sense her eyes have been opened as well as her ears. Thornton's chances with her in the short term have diminished; yet there is hope for him in her reaction and her motivation. She has saved him and revealed part of herself to herself.

Corn law rhymes Again by Ebenezer Elliott.
terrible wild beast . . . a troop of animals The insistent animal imagery suggests people dehumanized by suffering.
a film came over her eyes Mrs Gaskell is sometimes guilty of cliché, as here.

Chapter 23 Mistakes

Thornton enters, and is told that Margaret has gone home. Mrs Thornton tries to curb him by saying that Margaret has done what she did because she loves him, but this only excites him the more. He says that he will go to call on Margaret, and determines to do so the next day. He tells his mother that he intends to propose to Margaret. Meanwhile Margaret goes home after the riot, reassures her parents, then castigates herself for her behaviour. The water-bed arrives; Margaret lies down to sleep with her sense of shame.

Commentary

The aftermath is made dramatic with Thornton's barely contained passion for Margaret and the interaction with his mother, who is passionate, possessive but straight, able to admire what Margaret has done but capable only of putting one construction on it. There is a quality of pathos about the way she is prepared to yield up her son. The major emphasis in the chapter is on Margaret's reactions. There is some subtlety here, since she talks herself into believing that Thornton means nothing to her, whereas in fact, although she has acted on principle, she has also revealed her deep feeling for him. The refusal to acknowledge this to herself is understandable in the circumstances of her overhearing the servant's words. Margaret is still ruled by her pride, hence her reaction here.

Spenser Edmund Spenser (1552–99). The motto comes from *The Faerie Queene* (1590;1596).
the mêlée i.e. riotous brawl.

Chapter 24 Mistakes Cleared Up

Thornton comes to see Margaret. He is at once excited and apprehensive at the thought of what he has to say. Margaret puts him on the wrong foot by forbidding him to speak of gratitude. He speaks of his love – she responds from the icy coldness of being offended. She plays on the word 'gentleman' and denies that there was anything personal in what she did. Thornton chafes, and leaves hurriedly, though Margaret has tried to repair matters by mentioning her father.

Commentary

Margaret is weak in terms of her physical and mental state, and this is in part why she reacts as she does. Mrs Gaskell is mistress of this kind of emotional situation. Margaret is on the defensive, and does not really know herself anyway. The result is conflict, but it is conflict full of sexual passion and pride. The situation, with its emotional misunderstandings at the forefront, is tense with what is spoken as well as what is unspoken. Margaret's real feelings are present when, as Thornton leaves, she sees what she feels are unshed tears in his eyes.

William Fowler (1560–1612), a minor poet, this motto being from one of his sonnets.
Altogether she looked like some prisoner Again a cunningly prophetic note, for she is imprisoned by her conscience when later she tells the saving lie.

Chapter 25 Frederick

Margaret compares the two proposals she has received. She fears Thornton's 'enduring love'. She rouses herself and goes to see Bessy. The latter, who is much worse, tells her of Nicholas's suffering because of the activities of the knobsticks, which have undermined the committee instructions that the union members should be prepared to endure anything, but that they were not to use violence. Nicholas's position has been made worse by his quarrel with Boucher. This has greatly upset Bessy. At home the water-bed has made some improvement for Mrs Hale. Mr Hale is upset by talk of Frederick, but Mrs Hale persuades Margaret to write to Frederick, urging him to return quickly. Mr Hale has gone out, and only learns of this on his return.

Commentary

We are aware of Margaret's feelings for Thornton more strongly than she is. The fact is that she fears the strength of the man, who is essentially passionate by nature. The visit to Bessy takes her out of herself, and we realize the complications now of the strike action, with the knobsticks having succeeded by their violence in undermining the justice and the peacefulness of the Union's cause. Margaret has to adapt herself after her personal conflict to the much wider conflict that is now threatened. Meanwhile at home her responsibilities also increase with the importunate demands of her mother that she should write to Frederick. Her doing so despite her misgivings shows that Margaret senses that her father is incapable of action and that she must act, right or wrong.

Byron (1788–1824). Angus Easson unerlines the appropriateness of the motto by pointing out that it is from *The Island*, a poem which deals with the mutiny on the *Bounty*.

Fairfax's Tasso Edward Fairfax translated the famous Italian poet Tasso's *Gerusalemme Liberata* (an epic) in 1600. The line concerned reads 'Her sweet idea wander'd through his thought.'

Fais ce que dois Do what you ought to do, whatever happens.

settle A wooden seat for two or more people.

beyond my place i.e. exceeded my right.

a deep chap A thoughtful man.

physic-powder i.e. medicine in the form of powder.

peach Inform.

clapped up i.e. imprisoned.

purring an' a' (Dialect) kicking (with clogs on) and all.

the New Heavens, and the New Earth See Revelation, 21.

Chapter 26 Mother and Son

Thornton and his suffering reaction after Margaret's rejection, as he walks and tries to reconcile the differences in her character. He even takes an omnibus ride to try to get her out of his mind, but does not succeed. Meanwhile in the drawing-room his mother awaits his return, convinced that he will be accepted by Margaret. She broods on her resentment at the thought of Margaret usurping her position. When her son returns with his news she expresses her hate, but Thornton will not hear anything against Margaret, and in fact feels that he is not good enough for her.

Commentary

This chapter shows us the passionate nature of Thornton as he tries to reason with himself. Love has conquered him, so much so that he feels 'this miserable bodily pain' in his frustration. It is a remarkable study in obsession, for it is not until later in the day that he sufficiently recovers himself to attend to the immediate business of taking action with his brother magistrates against the offenders. Mrs Thornton's isolation is superbly conveyed. Her unpicking of the initials is an indication of her stoic acceptance of Margaret, though the irony is that Margaret has already rejected the son she is willing herself to part with. We are told that if Margaret had been a Milton girl Mrs Thornton would have liked her; she is also further mortified and despondent when she compares Margaret with Fanny. Thornton's return and his mother's impassioned responses – notice the strong family likeness between mother and son – are finely, economically, passionately focused. We feel for both. Thornton typically has re-course to the strike situation as panacea for what he has been through on the personal level with Margaret.

Mrs Hemans This quotation used in the motto is identified by Angus Easson as being from *The Bride of the Greek Isle*.
honour, love, obedience, troops of friends The reference is to *Macbeth*, Act V, Scene 3 – 'And that which should accompany old age/As honour, love, obedience, troops of friends'.
knock up Finish, bring to an end.

Chapter 27 Fruit-Piece

Thornton commands respect and takes decisions with regard to trade. After he has dispatched his magistrate's business he meets Dr Donaldson, who tells him of Mrs Hale's state. The result is that Thornton goes directly to her with a bunch of fruit. He ignores Margaret, who is present. A chance remark of her father's causes her to cry. Hot upon this comes word from Dixon that Mary has brought the news of Bessy's death.

Commentary

Mrs Gaskell is intent upon building up the full picture of Thornton, and we see him as the public man taking commercial and legal decisions, so that he is acting throughout with commendable responsibility. In some ways he complements Margaret in determination and character. But he is as impetuous and as warm as ever, and the purchase of the fruit shows the warmth and passion of the man being channelled into practical expressions of kindness. Margaret is injured by his social neglect, but before she has time to brood about it she has to act. Typically, she refuses to let Dixon go in her stead to see Bessy's body; it is a mark of her determination and character, and looks forward to her own ability to cope when her mother dies and her father and Frederick are unequal to the situation.

Midsummer Night's Dream Act V, Scene 1, 82–3 – the source of the
  motto.
the miller . . . Dee From *Love in a Village* (1762) by a minor writer,
Isaac Bickerstaffe.
carte-blanche i.e. a free hand.
crabs i.e. crab-apples.
crane's bill i.e. any of the plants of the geranium variety.
axed Asked.
somewhat Something.

Chapter 28 Comfort in Sorrow

Margaret takes her look at death, which she finds peaceful, and then has to reason with a violent Higgins, himself distraught by what has occurred. Mary pleads with her father not to drink, but it is Margaret who succeeds in restraining him. Higgins tells her of his day, then Margaret succeeds in taking him home with her to drink tea with her father. The latter is at first put out, but when he goes to see Higgins, Margaret, with Dixon's help, has to calm her mother, who is fretting at the thought of danger to Frederick. She need not have worried about her father and Higgins. They get on well together, apart from one violent hiccup on the question of faith. There follows a summary of the situation from the union point of view, with a reiteration of their being let down by the violence of some of their members. Higgins cites the way Hamper has treated him, and then defines the authoritarian power of the Union for the benefit of Margaret. She calls it tyranny. She, Higgins and her father pray.

Commentary

Most of this chapter speaks directly for itself. Mrs Gaskell has been accused of having too many deaths in her fiction, and certainly they come thick and fast from now on. We admire the way Margaret handles Higgins – she is being taken out of herself again – and parallels Thornton in her activity on behalf of others. Here she is the agent who is reconciling North and South or, more particularly, the classes and spiritual differences of men. Bessy is almost lost sight of in the action – but this is a reflection of the fact that death is cheap in industrial, deprived Victorian England. It must be allowed too that Mrs Gaskell is intent on reconciliation, and the account of the union solidarity is balanced by the tyranny of the employers and their blackmailing employment of Irish labour – though Mrs Gaskell does not pitch this strongly. The propagandist tone in this chapter some-how diminishes the humanity which is so much a part of Mrs Gaskell's concern. But it is a way of linking the social/industrial with the personal. After that final prayer Higgins goes home to his dead daughter, knowing that he is facing a bleak existence on both a private and a public level.

Kosegarten Mrs Browning Both mottoes are identified by Angus Easson (World's Classics edition p.443).
He giveth His Beloved sleep Revelation, 14, 13.
dwam (Dialect) faint.
gait Way.
ossed (Dialect) offered.
snug Safe.
Daniel O'Rourke . . . hook From a proverbial story of a drunken Irishman who found himself on the moon but refused to let go of his reaping-hook. It was chopped off and he fell into the sea.
pump-trough i.e. trough of water in the street.
the same fix i.e. the same situation.
varsal Universal.
dreed Suffered.
the fourteenth chapter of Job Concerned with the finality of the life-span of man.
It's save as save can i.e. everyone for himself.
th' overlooker The foreman.

larn Teach.
bolus A large pill (i.e. a continuation of the medical analogy Higgins has used in this paragraph).
The fathers have eaten sour grapes . . . set on edge See Ezekiel, 18,2.

Chapter 29 A Ray of Sunshine

The other south now re-enters the narrative – Edith's south, with its impractical invitation for Mrs Hale and Margaret to come and join her in her indolent life. Margaret reads the letter to her mother, but they are interrupted by Mr Thornton's arriving with another offering of fruit. He leaves quickly, 'with a grave farewell' as far as Margaret is concerned. Margaret talks to her mother, who really wants to be visited by Mrs Thornton. Later Mr Hale comes in accompanied by Thornton; Margaret tries to excuse what she has been saying in order not to offend Mr Thornton, but he does not understand her, and listens instead to what Mrs Hale is saying. Margaret behaves well towards Mr Thornton, but he has been deeply wounded by her. He promises Mrs Hale that his mother will call on her the next day.

Commentary

Edith's letter is seen in contrast to the intensely practical way of life Margaret is forced to embrace, both privately and in public. The real interaction in the chapter is between Margaret and Thornton; Mrs Gaskell is adept at entering the consciousness of each and, in Margaret's case, the conscience too. We notice too Mrs Hale's sensitivity; she wants to see Mrs Thornton for a particular purpose. It is the first time that she really looks outside herself. One of Mrs Gaskell's themes is that adversity brings out the best in people.

Coleridge The motto is quoted from one of his Notebooks.
the Peace Society Formed in England in 1816, avowed aim peace, with disputes settled by arbitration; anti-war, they attracted large crowds in the 1840s, hence the topicality of Mrs Gaskell's reference.
King Herod The King of Judaea who ordered the massacre of the Innocents.
slack of work i.e. has little work available to her.

Chapter 30 Home at Last

When Mrs Thornton pays her visit Mrs Hale is much worse, and this softens her, though her promise of help for Margaret – for this is Mrs

Hale's request – should she need it, is a qualified one. Frederick meanwhile is expected; Martha the servant is got out of the house so that she shall know nothing of it, and Margaret herself has to support Mr Hale. Frederick arrives, is greeted by Margaret, who takes him to his father. Later Dixon sees Frederick. The latter is taken to his mother. She dies in the night. It is Margaret who utters the prayer for the family.

Commentary

This is an example of Mrs Gaskell's cramming all she can get into one chapter. The contrast between Mrs Hale and Mrs Thornton is admirably done, with Mrs Hale's pathetic 'Call her Margaret' a wish to have her daughter loved. The irony is that one day Mrs Thornton will call her just that as her daughter-in-law. Both are strongly individualized in this scene, with Mrs Hale showing much more concern as she nears death than she did in life. The speed of Frederick's arrival, and of his mother's death, makes for narrative tension. Mrs Gaskell has now thoroughly involved the reader on a number of levels – the Margaret/Thornton affair, the strike, Frederick and Mrs Hale, Bessy, now dead, and Higgins. The adhesive is their interaction.

Southwell The poet Robert Southwell (1561–95).
Mrs Hemans See note p.18.
Poeta nascitur, non fit (Latin) the poet is born, not made.
Let not your heart be troubled See John, 14,1.

Revision questions on Chapters 21–30

1 What do you consider to be the most dramatic incident in these chapters and why?

2 Write an account of the feelings of Thornton and Margaret as they appear in these chapters.

3 Consider the parts played by Mrs Hale and Mrs Thornton in these chapters.

4 What are the immediate effects of Bessy's death, and what does it show us of Margaret's character?

5 Compare the behaviour of Mr Hale and Dixon in their reactions to Mrs Hale's illness and death.

Chapter 31 'Should auld Acquaintance be Forgot'

The woman pays, at least in the domestic sense, for after the death the work devolves upon Dixon and Margaret. Dixon gives the news that she has seen Leonards, who was on the Orion at the same time as Frederick. She urges Margaret to get Frederick away before he is recognized and captured. Leonards has already spoken to Dixon, not knowing where Frederick is exactly, urging her to help him trap Lieutenant Hale, as he calls him. Meanwhile, Mr Bell is to be contacted about the funeral. Thornton calls, but only Mr Hale sees him; he has come to offer any assistance he can give. Frederick now tells them of his love for Dolores Barbour, who is a Roman Catholic. Further discussion finds Margaret urging Frederick to put his case to Henry Lennox.

Commentary

Narrative tension is maintained in the best Victorian fashion, for with Dixon's news the fears for Frederick are increased. As ever, it is Margaret who is practical, both after the death of her mother and in seeking some way out for Frederick. The latter strikes one as being as egocentric as his parents, though he possesses some charm and some reflex warmth. Note that Frederick's snobbery over Thornton approximates to Margaret's, but that Margaret's character is deepening. There is pathos in the way she tries to ensure (a) that Frederick escapes and (b) that he takes legal advice, since she is losing her family – in the death of her mother and the unmanned grief, self-indulgent and weak, of her father.

Should Auld Acquaintance be Forgot The words of the chapter title are by Robert Burns (1759–96) from *Auld Lang Syne*.

Crabbe (1754–1832), the motto is from *The Borough*.

What a pity poor old Dixon . . . Just occasionally, as here, Frederick comes alive through his sense of humour.

au pied de la lettre Literally.

coursed i.e. followed out.

No mean brick . . . of my palace And it is this kind of language that makes Frederick unrealistic and, to use a word much in use today, chauvinistic.

Chapter 32 Mischances

Margaret begins to suffer the more as the other two get over their grief. Mr Hale is terrified that Frederick will be captured, and it is arranged that Margaret will accompany her brother to the station. Walking by the station with Frederick Margaret sees and is seen by Thornton; a little later, as the train approaches, Leonards sees Frederick by the light of the lamp. Frederick pushes him, and boards the train; afterwards, Margaret gets the down train. Leonards, who has only fallen a few feet, is thought by his fellow-workers to be drunk.

Commentary

The emphasis is once more on narrative speed and incident. Mr Hale is obsessed with the thought of his son being hanged, and this is the impetus for Frederick's quick removal from Milton. The plot sequence is further complicated by the appearance of Thornton, who does not know of Frederick's existence. The pushing of Leonards is itself dramatic; tension is set up in the reader. Is he injured? Has he recognised Margaret? Will he recover and pass information to the police? Since there is a reward involved, he will certainly try to. Mrs Gaskell wrote a number of stories which have just this kind of graphically dramatic situation: here she is using it in her novel to good effect.

Werner The motto is from the fifth act of the play of that name by Lord Byron (1823).
nearest vaults i.e. place to drink.
five shillings 25p today, but of course worth very much more at that time.

Chapter 33 Peace

Margaret decides not to say anything to her father. Her fear is that Leonards will follow Frederick to London. Mr Bell has gout and cannot come to the funeral. Margaret is upset because Mr Hale wants Thornton to go to the funeral with him, and further upset when the Thorntons offer their carriage. She is also worried by the fact that Frederick in London cannot make contact with Henry Lennox, who is out of town. Margaret goes with her father to the funeral; there she sees Higgins and Mary watching, while Thornton is there too and asks Dixon how they are. Thornton is inwardly jealous of the handsome stranger he saw with Margaret at the Outwood Station. Dixon does not tell Margaret of her interview with Thornton.

Commentary

The chapter has an ironic title, since the only one at peace is Mrs Hale. The narrative tension is still present, much depending on Margaret's pride and strength of character when she decides to accompany her father to the funeral rather than take up the Thorntons' generous offer. Much of the dramatic effect from now on depends on misunderstanding (Thornton thinking that Frederick is Margaret's lover) or on lack of communication (Dixon's not telling Margaret of her conversation with Thornton). Margaret has to bear up in public, thus drawing on her reserves of strength. Thornton is in the same position, and his inner turmoil is described as 'the Charybdis of passion'.

Dr King (1592–1669); the motto quotes from a poem on his wife.
strait Trial, endurance.
the Charybdis of passion A ship-devouring whirlpool in classical mythology, opposite Scylla, the rock thought to wreck sailors, both in the straits of Messina.

Chapter 34 False and True

They do not hear from Frederick when they expect to; Thornton pays them a visit. Margaret is moved, but she is called out by Dixon, who tells her that a police-inspector has come to see her. Margaret learns that Leonards is dead, but denies that she was at the Outwood station on the evening concerned. She has been provisionally if vaguely identified by a grocer's assistant. The inspector tells her that he may have to visit her again. Margaret goes into the study, and faints.

Commentary

This is the stuff of melodramatic story-telling, elevated to a pitch of intensity by the character of Margaret and by the inward examination of her conscience. This is exposed almost between the lines of the inspector's questions. For Margaret to tell a lie is an effort of the will, so much so that she is physically shattered by the experience. The tension is added to by the reader's knowledge that Mr Hale and Mr Thornton are so near; this is what makes Margaret's simple and repetitive lies such a burden. It is almost as if she is in a trance from which there is no release. From her situation there *is* no release until Frederick is away and safe.

Anon (Rhyme scheme as in *In Memoriam*).
She fixed him with her eye An echo of the practice of Coleridge's Ancient Mariner.
Cornish trick i.e. a hold in wrestling, Cornishmen being noted for their prowess at this sport.
a hundred pounds poorer i.e. because he had lost the reward money.

Chapter 35 Expiation

Mr Thornton is a great comfort to Mr Hale as they sit, and Mr Hale confides in him. They become closer to each other as a result. Gradually, in the study, Margaret recovers consciousness, knowing that she will have to confess once she is assured that Frederick is safe. When Thornton goes into the street the inspector tells him of the situation; he is astounded to hear (though he keeps it to himself) of Margaret's denial that she was at the station. Thornton tells him not to do anything until he has seen him again. He takes upon himself to save Margaret by saying that there will be no inquest. The inspector returns having been told this, and then calls on Margaret. He reads Thornton's note to her.

Margaret's agony begins when the inspector has gone. She now knows that Thornton knows she is a liar. There is worse to come, since all this could have been avoided, for Frederick's letter arrives, having been posted too late to save her from her own moral and legal perjury. She prays long and hard, and afterwards with her secret knowledge she is treated with great tenderness by her father. He even plans for her to go to Spain to see Frederick's beloved Dolores. Meanwhile Margaret has one comfort in her despondency – the respect that she feels for Mr Thornton. Her pride asserts itself when Thornton sends to know how her father is – she refuses to let any message be sent back which says how *she* is.

Commentary

Narrative immediacy, swift movement and change, these are the main constituents of this chapter. There is the element of chance – Leonards' death, the delay in Frederick's letter – and the fine and moving structural parallels between the state of Margaret and the state of Thornton. How far each complements the other in love is remarkable, even down to the *saving lie*. Mrs Gaskell is adroitly balancing the sensational narrative with the human. Thornton's love at this stage is the more extreme and impassioned because acknowledged; Margaret's is secret and concealed even from herself, since she takes refuge in a word like 'respect' to convey her feelings. Once again Mrs Gaskell has managed to get a number of incidents into the chapter; the coming together of Thornton and Mr Hale is true to life, and Mr Hale's tenderness to Margaret after all she has gone through (with the irony that he doesn't know all she has gone through) shows Mrs Gaskell's constant human awareness. Narrative interest is high – now we must read on always with the knowledge that Thornton and Margaret, like masters and men, will come together.

There's nought . . . the sun The theme of this quotation in the motto is that all will be revealed, a comment in itself on Margaret's saving lie.

Of death . . . grown dull Editors have failed to trace the source of this quotation.

E par che de la sua labbia si mova (Italian) 'It seems as if a sweet spirit of love comes from her lips, saying to the soul, Sigh!'

a dog, and done this thing 'But I am a dog, a mere nobody, how can I do this great thing'.

protégé i.e. one whom he had helped, put forward.

her lips were baked and livid still Note the unsparing realism of this phrases.

a packet A small ship.

Fais ce que dois . . . See note p.45.

Chapter 36 Union Not Always Strength

The next day Margaret and her father visit Higgins. He is out of work, though he has some money which Bessy had saved. Higgins has not asked for work, and he explains the post-strike situation. He reasserts his belief in the Union despite its authoritarian stance. Boucher has asked for work but has been turned away by Hamper. Shortly after this they hear outside the movement of tramping feet and noise; the men are bringing Boucher's body, for he has succeeded in drowning himself in a few inches of water. Again Margaret has to act, this time to comfort the widow and her children.

Commentary

There is a genuine pathos about Higgins's situation. The parallel of loss with the Hales' is stressed, but Mrs Gaskell now seems intent upon piling anguish on anguish. Almost immediately after Higgins has damned Boucher for his mealy-mouthed attitude the body is brought home. Immediately after Mrs Boucher has complained to Margaret about her husband's behaviour she learns that he is dead. Mrs Gaskell is showing cause, effect and human suffering at one and the same moment, underlining her theme that in the midst of life we are in death. The union situation shows Mrs Gaskell penetrating to the heart of the social matter – perhaps the divisions here are worse than they were before. It has become a commonplace of these Notes to refer to Margaret's courage – here, in her dealing with Mrs Boucher, particularly her fetching the baby to her, she shows a natural practical compassion and sensitivity that is warm and directly understanding.

Shelley (1792–1822), major English Romantic Poet. The motto is a slight misquotation from *The Sensitive Plant*.

habiliments i.e. mourning clothes.

I'll bide inside . . . That's a' i.e. if she takes any money from you, I won't let her enter the house.

making an ado . . . could sarve yo' i.e. kicking up a fuss, making much of the little that Mary could do for you.

true to yo'r order i.e. loyal to your beliefs.

turn-outs fro' clemming i.e. strikers from starving.

ossing Offering.

pinch i.e. deprivation, suffering.

used for dyeing purposes Note that this makes Boucher's death all the more grotesque.

We'n done a deal i.e. we've done our share.

felled Stricken.

ill-redd-up i.e. cleaned in a slovenly way

mithering (Dialect) worrying, fretting.

butties Bread slices with butter or treacle etc.

calling him i.e. criticising.

whisth Hush, quiet.

Chapter 37 Looking South

Margaret and her father go to the Bouchers. Higgins is away from home. They try to cope with the misery of Mrs Boucher and to turn the children towards practical activity. Margaret continues to brood on her lie. Later Higgins comes to see them. He has been in search of work so that he can help to support Boucher's widow and children. He has come to ask them what his prospects would be in the South, but Margaret points him in the direction of Thornton. She realizes that it would be impossible for him to get work in the South, but she has come to a new respect for the determination of these northerners, observing that 'There's granite in all these northern people, papa, is there not?'.

Commentary

There is some keen insight into the psychology of poverty and too much childbearing in the portrait of Mrs Boucher. Touching too is the response of the children, who were fond of their father. We cannot help thinking of the querulousness of Mrs Hale in her adversity and the terrible adversity of Mrs Boucher which has virtually destroyed her human responses. Higgins shows his real humanity, for he has sunk his pride and is to sink it even more by taking Margaret's advice and going to Thornton. It is not merely his granite, it is the morality that makes him feel guilty and responsible that is driving him on. Adversity, guilt, these are pivotal in Mrs Gaskell's work, and out of Margaret's guilt over her lie comes the genuine appraisal of people and, more keenly, her appreciation of Thornton.

Hood (Thomas Hood, 1799–1845), is quoted in the motto from *The Lay of the Labourer*.
redding (Dialect) tidying.
a strange kind of way i.e. he seems to be behaving oddly.
Sarvant i.e. your servant (a polite form of address).
the bits o' childre i.e. the small children.
o' th' road i.e. I pushed him in that direction.
Theer's ne'er a man, to call a man i.e. no one worthy of the name of a man (an interesting analogy with the use of the word by Thornton).
spade Dig.
I'se nought particular i.e. I don't have to have (my meat).
rucks (Dialect) plenty.
fettling (Dialect) working out properly, putting to rights.
nesh Weak, feeble.
as lief stand on my own bottom I'd just as soon be independent.

Chapter 38 Promises Fulfilled

We now switch to Thornton's reactions. He believes that Margaret has a lover, and he 'lashed himself into an agony of fierce jealousy'. Mrs Thornton notices her son's disquiet, and through the story of one of her servants, probes her son about Margaret's presence at the station on the night in question. She is mindful of her promise to Mrs Hale to do the right thing by Margaret. Thornton himself is convinced that Margaret is in some trouble. Mrs Thornton calls on

Margaret, performs her duty, accuses her of impropriety; Margaret tells her that she (Mrs Thornton) does not understand the situation, and finally sweeps out of the room. While this is happening Higgins goes to Thornton to request work. One of Thornton's employees points out who Higgins is. Higgins humbles himself on Boucher's family's account, but Thornton rejects him. At the same time he marvels that the man has waited to see him for five hours.

Commentary

The switch to Thornton further underlines the passionate nature of the man. His moodiness at home provokes Mrs Thornton's actions, though perhaps the coincidence that Betsy was engaged to Leonards is a little too much to take. The study of mother and son is brilliantly focused – despite his jealousy he really cares for Margaret, and Mrs Thornton cares for her son in such a way that she almost enjoys doing her duty and keeping her word to Mrs Hale. The confrontation with Margaret is impressively handled, with Margaret at bay as she was with the police inspector, but now with the additional burden of being suspected of impropriety. One of Mrs Gaskell's great strengths is her ability to humanize in small compass. Mrs Thornton goes somewhat 'over the top' in her picture of her son's suffering and the fact that he is too good for Margaret, but she is redeemed by seeing the ludicrousness of her position when Margaret leaves her alone. The second confrontation, that between Thornton and Higgins, is even better, the dialogue and dialect ringing completely true. Thornton is as unpleasant as he needs to be in view of the supposed nature of the man he is seeing; but Higgins has come a long way in humanity from the gruff and defensive person we first met. The hope for the future reconciliation – or at least the prospect of differences being resolved and of masters and men working together – is seen in Thornton's pondering on Higgins's long wait. The human element is Mrs Gaskell's – and Margaret's – concern, and both Thornton and Higgins are here displaying a deepening human awareness.

Scotch ballad The only identification of the extract used in the motto.
an offended princess Typical of the imagery used of Margaret.
beau i.e. young man.
a Paddy that didna know weft fro' warp i.e. an Irishman who didn't know anything about cotton-production.

Chapter 39 Making Friends

Margaret by herself, brooding on Mrs Thornton's words but proud too that Thornton has not even told his mother what he obviously feels. She walks out, meets her father on her return, then goes to Mrs Boucher's. The latter is dying. Nicholas is there, and tells her of his rejection by Thornton. Margaret has just said that she is disappointed in Thornton when the latter appears. Margaret leaves, but Thornton begs Higgins's pardon for having doubted him, and offers him work. They agree to see how they get on. Later Thornton overtakes Margaret, tells her that her secret is safe with him, but will not go on walking with her because she will not confide in him, and anyway, he no longer feels himself in love with her. Although Margaret answers this sadly and they part, she throws herself into merriment and seeks to free herself from her reactions to Thornton by thinking about the future.

Commentary

The human movement noticed in the previous chapter is markedly present in the first part of this one, though the coincidence smacks of contrivance rather than realism. That Thornton should appear immediately after Margaret's words and that he should beg Nicholas's pardon seems to partake of the ideal rather than the real. Having said that, it is a very effective scene, and it says much for Thornton's character that he has sought out Nicholas. His softening here is even qualified by humour; in fact the two men's appraisal of each other contains just enough respect and doubt to make it possible that they will get on. When Thornton and Margaret talk we are aware of the subtlety and accuracy of Mrs Gaskell's presentation; Thornton believes, or would have Margaret believe, that he no longer loves her. Margaret believes that she can put Thornton out of her mind. Each is palpably, culpably, wrong.

Drayton Michael Drayton (1563–1631), from his Sonnet which begins, 'Since there's no help, come let us kiss and part.'
Never yo' fret i.e. don't you concern yourself.
marcy Mercy.
rayther have me 'bout my brains Rather have me without my intelligence.
She was more roused by a letter from Edith This whole section indicates how little Margaret knows herself – she thinks she wants Harley Street, but in reality she wants Thornton.

Chapter 40 Out of Tune

Mr Bell arrives, and proves to be a lively character with a good sense of humour and an immediate fondness for Margaret. Meanwhile Thornton, who has not had any words with his mother about her meeting with Margaret, visits the Hales for tea, and is all ears when he hears Henry Lennox's name mentioned. During the conversation Mr Bell reveals that Margaret has become pro-Milton in her attitudes. This is naturally a surprise to Mr Thornton. He gives offence by a sarcastic comment on Margaret's reputation for truthfulness. After he has gone, Mr Bell, who is nothing if not astute, asks Mr Hale if there is something between Thornton and Margaret. Nicholas tells Margaret that Thornton is interested in Boucher's children. But Margaret is conscious that they have grown away from the Thorntons, and Thornton himself begins to neglect his lessons with her father.

Commentary

Mr Bell has a fine, if somewhat acid and sarcastic sense of humour. Interaction between Margaret and Thornton is conditioned by the tension they feel in each other's company. The fact that he feels passion and that she confesses to her father shows the deep hold which each has on the other despite their outward behaviour. If Mr Bell is astute, then so is Higgins; he sees the essential division in Mr Thornton between the private and the public man. There is a sense of isolation and distance at the end of the chapter.

Wyatt Sir Thomas Wyatt (?1503–42) the author of the lines used in the motto.

he dreamt she came dancing towards him . . . Note the element of wish-fulfilment in this dream, which is relatively straightforward compared with Margaret's about Henry Lennox.

the Una from the Duessa From Spenser's *The Faerie Queene*, with Una representing purity and true religion, Duessa evil.

the Kilkenny' cat's tail Another Irish story, this time about two cats who fought until they only had their tails and claws left.

the Heptarchy The combined kingdoms of the Angles and Saxons.

Thor God of the Scandinavians.

her rocking it, and rating it Quoted from Richard Edwards (?1523–66) in his *Paradise of Dainty Devices* (1576).

tendresse i.e. were in love with one another.

Prince Camaralzaman . . . Princess Badoura Their love story in *The Arabian Nights*, after they have been brought together because of their perfections by genii, is initially a troubled one, but they are happy in the end. In some ways they parallel Margaret and Thornton.

Where's the Pearl? 'Margaret' is from the Greek name for 'pearl'.

all o'er In every way.

craddy (Dialect) puzzle.

caught in some of the zones i.e. one of the tropical areas.

now he has sold out i.e. paid to be released from his commission.

Revision questions on Chapters 31–40

1 In what ways does Margaret assume even more responsibility than hitherto? Refer closely to the text in your answer.

2 Describe what led to Margaret's telling the saving lie and her reasons for doing it.

3 'Thornton is guilty of moral dishonesty.' Discuss.

4 Write an account of the events immediately after Boucher's death.

5 Indicate the parts played by Higgins and Mrs Thornton in these chapters.

Chapter 41 The Journey's End

They go on through the winter, Margaret hearing occasionally of Thornton, who pays them four visits, but she is somewhat depressed. In March Frederick marries, having previously learned that there was little hope of a pardon. Mr Hale goes to visit Mr Bell in Oxford in April. Margaret quietly discovers that the way out of herself is to take the way of humility. Then she learns that Fanny is to marry an older but very prosperous man. She continues to teach Boucher's children. Meanwhile in Oxford the round of visits has fatigued Mr Hale. Mr Bell reveals that he intends to care for Margaret and to make provision for her. Mr Hale dies, and Mr Bell sets out to tell Margaret the sad news. On the train he meets Thornton and tells him. He also implies that Margaret will probably choose to live with her London relations. The chapter ends with Margaret's guessing what has happened when she sees Mr Bell.

Commentary

In fact this chapter marks the passage of time and the changes which it brings. It is ironic that as soon as Margaret determines to get out of herself her father's death brings an added burden to her. The marriages of Frederick and Fanny are neither of them surprises, since both are egoists intent on doing the best for themselves. Mr Bell, even in these troubles, has a delicious tongue-in-cheek humour when he confides his plans to Thornton, but fears that he may be caught by the aunt (Mrs Shaw). Mr Thornton is obviously having a struggle to keep going, but we note Higgins's respect for him and Margaret's natural Christian reflex of helping the Boucher children.

Browning's Paracelsus (Robert Browning 1812–89), *Paracelsus* (1835), Part 1, lines 560–65.
unnative himself Unusual way of putting the fact that Frederick is rejecting his own country.
preux chevalier (French) gallant knight.
Je ne voudrois pas reprendre . . . I should not like to blame my heart in this way. Die of shame in your blind, impudent and deceitful disloyalty to your God and such things: but I would wish to put it right through compassion, saying, Now, my poor heart, we are tumbled here into the pit which we had determined to escape. Ah! Let us search for the light and depart from this pit for ever. Let us beg the mercy of God and hope that it will help us from now on to be stronger; let us seek once again the path of humility. Courage, may we be on our guard in the future. God will help us. (Francis de Sales, 1567–1622.)
away Begin.
the car of the conqueror i.e. being obsessed by Margaret.
preux chevalier See note above.
pis aller Last resort.

Chapter 42 Alone! Alone!

Margaret is too ill with shock and grief to be moved. Despite the fact that Edith is expecting her second child, Mr Bell peremptorily requests the pleasure of Mrs Shaw's company to comfort Margaret. With her arrival, Margaret is of course reminded of her mother. Mrs Shaw wants to take her back home, Mr Bell moves out to stay with Mr Thornton, and Fanny prepares ostentatiously for her wedding. Mr Bell lets slip the name of Frederick and his part in the mutiny; Thornton asks if Frederick has been to England but Bell answers in the negative. He gives Thornton to understand that it was probably Henry Lennox that he saw walking with Margaret. Thornton resents Bell's tone when he asks him if he loves Margaret, but the subject is changed and Thornton reveals that he has built a dining-room for the men, largely because of his conversations with Higgins. In terms of human relationships, things are now working out well between master and men.

Commentary

Again there is a noticeable speed of movement in this chapter. Mr Bell's action in writing to Mrs Shaw shows his strength of character and his sense of justice. We note the thorough-going selfishness of Edith and the indolent self-interest of Henry Lennox. Mrs Shaw brings to Milton the same snobbish prejudices as did her sister and her niece, and the misunderstandings continue with Bell's account of Frederick and the probability of Lennox being in Milton. Mrs Gaskell, ever intent on her theme of reconciliation, has Thornton introduce his canteen venture. Higgins, Thornton and Margaret are all moving more directly into humanitarian involvement; despite this, there are times when Mr Bell's wit blows like a breath of fresh air across these sombre situations.

Mrs Browning From her sonnet *Substitution*.
vis inertiae (Latin) natural indolence.
cutting open the pages of a new Review Books and magazines at this time were often 'uncut' at the top of the page.
savoir-faire Ability to do the right thing regardless of circumstances.
'station' i.e. her position in society.
win yo' come Will you join us?

Chapter 43 Margaret's Flittin'

Captain Lennox and Thornton go to the funeral with Bell, who writes Margaret a sensible letter. He tells her that she is to inherit his money when he dies, and virtually dictates the terms on which she is to stay with her aunt Shaw who, naturally, cannot stand Milton. Margaret makes her preparations, sending one of her father's books to Thornton and paying her farewells despite her aunt's objections. She takes a remembrance of Bessy, calls on Mrs Thornton who treats her with justice (Mrs Shaw treats Mrs Thornton with insensitivity), and says an outwardly calm goodbye to Thornton. Perhaps it is fitting that a determined and much happier Nicholas Higgins should be the last to see her. He appreciates her as much as anybody.

Commentary

The divisions between north and south are still present in the persons of Mrs Shaw and Mrs Thornton. But this is a moving chapter, for Margaret forces herself to do all that she knows she should do and wants to do. She is right, and the condescension of Mrs Shaw cannot undermine her. There is a superb placing by Mrs Gaskell of the Thornton/Margaret goodbye exactly at the spot where she had tried to protect him. At this moment and immediately afterwards we feel Thornton's inner tumult, though we sense that he is being wrong-headed (though never wrong-hearted).

Elliott See note p.41.
summut Something.
let who will be t'other i.e. whoever the other good man may be.
butter me An exclamation of strong feeling (well, I'll be damned).
the deuce's own scribble i.e. written by the devil.

Chapter 44 Ease Not Peace

All goes smoothly in Harley Street though, strangely, Margaret even begins to think of Milton as home. She is left alone much during this London season, hears from Dixon who is winding up the family affairs in Milton, and then has a sudden visit from Mr Bell. He reveals that he has travelled up with Henry Lennox. He talks to Margaret, who reveals to him that Frederick was indeed in England and that Henry Lennox has been trying to help him. Mr Bell has escaped from the Thorntons largely because of the oppression of Fanny's wedding preparations. Margaret dislikes the idea of being left alone with Henry Lennox; Mr Bell stays long enough to meet Edith and Mrs Shaw. He leaves with Henry Lennox, to whom he takes a strong dislike because of his superficial and self-interested attitudes. Lennox is critical of Mr Hale's decision to leave the church, and this sets Mr Bell against him even more strongly.

Commentary

The changed Margaret is responding, or rather not responding, to the familiarity of Harley Street. The fact is that her life experiences, her involvement with working people, with class divisions and, above all, her having known grief and as yet unacknowledged love, has given her a distaste for this kind of indolence. But basically this chapter fills in another detail in the plot – the fact that Mr Bell has misinformed Thornton about Frederick's not being in England. We are invited to contemplate the selfish superficiality and self-indulgence of the South; and with Margaret we think back with some longing to the North. Margaret is beginning to discover herself. Mr Bell follows no process of discovery. He knows already what Mrs Shaw and Edith are like – he cleverly employs euphemisms to cover his feelings – and he intuitively knows what Henry Lennox is like. That petty egoist reveals himself for what he is – a shallow, small opportunist of a man.

Cowper William Cowper (1731–1800). This quotation is from 'Hope'.
Ruckert Friedrich Rückert (1781–1866), German poet.
Vashti See Esther, 1. She was the Queen who refused to accept her husband's commands when they were delivered by a chamberlain.
du billet i.e. as a writer of notes.
impromptu i.e. arranged quickly, prepared at short notice.
smoke-dried i.e. bringing the industrial smoke of the town with him.
and threw the ball back i.e. responded to what he had said.
Mordecai See Esther, 2 and 3. Esther was Mordecai's adopted daughter.
Don Quixote The idealistic and ridiculous hero of the novel *Don Quixote de la Mancha* by the great Spanish writer Cervantes.

Chapter 45 Not All a Dream

Margaret now learns from Henry Lennox that there is no hope for Frederick. Mr Bell reads her reactions carefully and then suggests that they go to Helstone the next day. She is delighted, and he easily gets round Aunt Shaw.

Commentary

This very short chapter is a further mark of Margaret's dissatisfaction with Harley Street life. She snatches at Helstone. Mr Bell's wit is still in evidence, and Mrs Shaw shows that she has no real character because she has no real concern.

W. S. Landor (1775–1864). From one of his epigrams.
lachrymal ducts Tear ducts.

Chapter 46 Once and Now

The journey to Helstone by train is described. When they arrive at the Lennard Arms (note the curious choice of name in view of Leonards) the landlady recognizes Margaret. She has not heard of Mr Hale's death. The landlady tells Mr Bell of the changes in the village since the Hales left. Margaret notices changes, but is intent on seeing little Susan, who was so upset when she left Helstone. She sees Susan's mother, learns that Susan has gone to the village school, and learns too that Betty Barnes has been guilty, from misguided superstition, of roasting a cat. She finds the school being run, efficiently and by the book, by the new Vicar's wife. The parsonage too is completely changed. Margaret finds herself going back into her other past. She tells Mr Bell the whole story of Frederick and how she fears Mr Thornton's assumption have made him cease to respect her. It is her confession; Mr Bell responds to it, and Margaret realizes that, though Helstone is important to her, its associations with her parents mean that she would not wish to visit it again.

Commentary

This is an important contribution to the education of Margaret's feelings. She has looked forward to re-entering the idyll – instead she is faced with the reality of change. That change is not just outward, it is inward too. This focus on Margaret embodies Mrs Gaskell's wisdom about life. Nothing is ever what we thought it was. The important germinating effect of this return is that it moves her to confession, and this can only do her good. There may also be a secret wish, unexpressed because of her pride, that Mr Bell may be able to help. In one superb passage Mrs Gaskell pinpoints Margaret's depression and sense of loss but also conveys the continuum of life through the burning of 'a candle in her old bedroom'. It is the sign of hope.

Uhland Johann Ludwig Uhland (1787–1862). German lyric poet.
London and North-Western Before the nationalization of the railways they were run by companies that operated in the various regions.
Herman and Dorothea Poem by Goethe (1749–1832) famous German poet and philosopher.
Evangeline Long poem by Henry Wadsworth Longfellow (1807–82).
fly Carriage.
I plunged some fresh-gathered roses Here an unobtrusive use of the symbol, ironic in view of Margaret's coming reactions to Helstone.
receipts i.e. recipes.
old trees had been felled Symbols of death, the death of Margaret's parents and in part of her past.

for simple Susan's sake See Angus Easson's note (p.447) of the World's Classics edition of *North and South*.

fat and scant o' breath An echo from the final scene in *Hamlet*.

But as my mother has not murdered my father Mr Bell is wittily distorting the plot of *Hamlet* – Hamlet's uncle kills his brother, Hamlet's father, and then marries Hamlet's mother.

thridded i.e. threaded.

Your father, I presume A wonderfully ironic note struck by Mrs Gaskell here.

a straw-hat forced down upon a rose-tree Brilliant use of symbol – Margaret would have treasured the roses as she treasured the past – both are damaged now.

Honi soit qui mal y pense (French) evil to him who evil thinks. (The motto of the Order of the Garter.)

as the fisherman coaxed the genie Another *Arabian Nights* reference.

Gerald Griffin's beautiful lines See Angus Easson's note, p.447.

From everlasting to everlasting See Hebrews, 13,8.

if that is not Irish i.e. if that is not silly.

Chapter 47 Something Wanting

Dixon brings Margaret all the Milton news, particularly about Thornton's purchases at the sale of their effects. Margaret hopes that Mr Bell will get in touch with Thornton, but his letters are short and irritable. Edith is frightened that Margaret will go to see her brother at Cadiz in the autumn. Margaret becomes attached to Edith's boy. She is aware of Henry Lennox.

Commentary

This is an updating chapter in the sense that we now know Margaret's state of mind. This is Mrs Gaskell's way of obliquely preparing us to know the state of Thornton's. Our interest is aroused by his absence from the narrative. The selfishness of Edith and her possessiveness over Margaret are again indicated. Margaret's awareness of Henry Lennox is inconclusive, but it is obvious to the reader that at this stage he cannot bring himself to be committed. It needs Mr Bell's leaving everything to Margaret to point Mr Lennox more determinedly in her direction.

Mrs Browning See note p.20. This motto is from one of her sonnets.

Chateau en Espagne i.e. Castle in Spain.

blue-sashed moods i.e. when he was dressed up.

keen-sighted, far-seeing . . . proud Note the fine antithetical balance through contrast that Mrs Gaskell achieves here.

Chapter 48 Ne'er to be Found Again

The dinner parties of Edith described. Henry Lennox begins to pay Margaret some attention, but always his cleverness rather than his sincerity is stressed. Meanwhile Mr Bell writes to say that he will shortly be coming up to town. Edith upbraids Margaret with wanting to go to Spain. Then Mr Bell has suddenly died. Margaret and Captain Lennox go to Oxford. She comes back to London and contemplates life and her own sins from the room where she had spent her girlhood.

Commentary

The opening of the chapter is finely ironic, the nature of the superficiality being defined through the account of the parties and the way they are formed. Once more there is an accretion of incident, though Mr Bell's death comes rather too suddenly to convince the reader. The final sequence from Margaret's consciousness, her determination to assert her integrity and to tell only the truth, is given a thoroughly convincing basis of faith. In moments of crisis throughout the novel Margaret has either turned to her faith, expressed it or explored it, and here she has found herself after all her tribulations.

Anon Author unidentified, but the motto fits the chapter content.
sans peur et sans reproche (French) without fear and free from reproach.

Chapter 49 Breathing Tranquillity

Edith discussing Margaret's inheritance, exchanges a few words with Henry Lennox on his chances with her; he is biding his time before he commits himself. Margaret goes to Cromer, not Spain, and is still brooding about Thornton's opinion of her. But 'all this time for thought' allows Margaret the chance to get everything into perspective. Meanwhile Lennox is determined to win her, and is planning ahead. He praises Milton and its inhabitants to her (after all, that's where her wealth is). Margaret is determined to follow where duty calls. Edith and Mrs Shaw keep eligible young men out of her way in order to further Henry's chances.

Commentary

The selfishness of the Shaw-cum-Lennox clan is exemplified here in the plans they lay for Margaret. I have referred elsewhere to the

opportunism of Henry Lennox; here he reveals in his forward planning unscrupulousness and cunning, which further condition our
unsympathetic response to him. Margaret's communion with herself
shows just how distanced she is from her relations. They have no
conception of what she is thinking. Mrs Gaskell is here subtly
expressing through her character the woman problem – what can an
intelligent woman with a sense of moral and social responsibility do in
life, if she doesn't marry? Of course the irony is that Henry Lennox
thinks that she will marry – but one thing is sure, she will not marry
him.

Hood Thomas Hood (1799–1845), English poet and humorist. The motto
is a quotation from his poem *Hero and Leander*.
farouche Shy, fierce.
Zenobia She ruled Palmyra, invaded Egypt and asia Minor, but was
defeated by the Roman Emperor Aurelian.
Cleopatra The ruler of Egypt, mistress notably of Julius Caesar and of
Mark Antony.

Chapter 50 Changes at Milton

The decline in Milton is spelt out. Thornton is hard pressed. His
ambitions have not been realized, while the strike, now eighteen
months in the past, had stopped him from fulfilling some of the orders
on hand. Higgins meets him one day and asks if he has heard anything
of Margaret. She is now Thornton's landlord, but the conversation
continues and Higgins recurs to the presence of Frederick in England.
Thornton is glad, but his public business is such that although he can
pay off all his employees he hasn't the capital to run it. He has been
offered a speculation, but turns it down on the grounds that if it failed
the money rightfully belonging to others would have been lost.
Thornton appeals to his mother for her spiritual support in this time
of crisis. Thornton becomes a manager, and his brother-in-law is soon
a rich man as a result of his speculation.

Commentary

The mixture is of small but important joy for Thornton in his
knowledge that Margaret was with Frederick, and large emphasis on
his integrity which withstands temptation. Mrs Gaskell's respect is
wholly given to her hero and his decision, for she writes bitterly of 'the
deep selfishness of competition'. The gradual coming together is still

concentrated on Higgins, for we are told that he and Thornton had led parallel lives. Perhaps there will only be this parallelism of interest and humanity rather than any merging, at least in Mrs Gaskell's mind. Higgins's revealing the truth about Frederick smacks of contrivance; it must be revealed since it is so important to the plot. The scene between Thornton and his mother is one of the finest in the book, she with her intense love and pride, he with a new-found humility and a sense, like Margaret, of spiritual being. As he says to his mother, 'If you would say the good old words, it would make me feel something of the pious simplicity of my childhood.' Mrs Thornton is deeply moved, and in this moment of terrible adversity realizes that the mere fact that he exists is the most important thing in her life. Mrs Gaskell's sense of financial evil and manipulation is shown in the final paragraph of the chapter. Fanny's older husband is a success in the superficial way that the world measures success – through the gaining of money. The irony of this in the context of Thornton's dedication and integrity is apparent.

we have all of us one human heart From Wordsworth's *The Old Cumberland Beggar*.
to potter him i.e. to worry him.
fretted his woman's heart out The implication is that Mr Hale was easily moved at the prospect of suffering in others, as easily moved as a woman.
ca'ed Called.

Chapter 51 Meeting Again

Edith has words with Dixon about flowers, and reveals to Margaret that Henry is bringing Thornton to dinner. Margaret does not like this but meets Thornton, who, though rather careworn, greets her as an old friend. She, however, is constrained. Edith, at first put out at having her number altered by Thornton's addition, realizes that he is much respected. To her own delight, Margaret realizes this too. Thornton impresses Colthurst, and refers to his 'experiments' in developing relationships with his men. His only approach to Margaret is to tell her that he has had a round-robin from some of his men saying that they would work for him again if the opportunity arose. He thinks that it is in Higgins's handwriting. Margaret tells Henry Lennox that she wishes to see him the next day since she wants his help 'about something'.

Commentary

The ironic presentation of Edith continues – to have the right number at a dinner-party is *so* important – but we are intent on the interaction between Margaret and Thornton. What Mrs Gaskell is so accurately depicting is the outward manner of person to person and how it is so easy for that manner to be misinterpreted. For Thornton to be held in such great respect seems a little fortuitous to say the least, since failure is the measure by which such a man is judged in his competitive world. But Mrs Gaskell is concerned that right and integrity should triumph, and it is obviously going to. We are moved when Thornton appeals to Margaret, and delighted at the end of the chapter, for we sense that Henry Lennox's expectations are wide of the mark.

garniture Decoration.
mot Witty remark or saying
apropos Pertinent.
cash nexus i.e. connected only by money.
the point Archimedes sought . . . 'Give me a point on which to stand, and I will move the earth.' The Greek mathematician, interested in the use of the lever, is here being linked to impossible ideas.
with her speaking eyes A fine phrase to convey Margaret's silent eloquence.

Chapter 52 'Pack Clouds Away'

Edith on tenterhooks the next day, but Henry soon disillusions her. The following day Lennox is supposed to meet Thornton and Margaret there – something to do with Thornton's lease – but fails to turn up. Thornton explains to Margaret why he wishes to give up his lease, though he says he does not want to hear Lennox's opinion of his affairs. Margaret takes the boldest step of her life, pointing out that Lennox has drawn up a proposal that her unused money should be lent to Thornton to enable him to re-work Marlborough Mills. He is moved to make his passionate assertion, and Margaret responds. Thornton reveals that he has been to Helstone to get the roses which he now shows her.

Commentary

This is a finely economical ending to the novel. The discomfiting of Henry Lennox, and to a certain degree of Edith, is sudden but effective. Margaret's idea of her duty, which had caused her so much deliberation, is here translated into courageous fact; that is her taking the lead after an inward self-recognition of her love for Thornton. His reaction is impassioned, and indeed the sexuality of the scene is unswervingly strong despite the reticence of the convention in which Mrs Gaskell writes. The novel ends on a note of delightful humour; each realizes the problems in their marriage, both social and personal. The woman has come through to play the major part in bringing that marriage about.

Pack Clouds Away The chapter title is derived from the Song by Thomas Heywood (1574–1641) in his play *The Rape of Lucrece*.

Do you know these roses? The final mention of this symbolic identification with Margaret, the ironic note being struck since she does not recognize them – they are part of the past and she is now living for the present.

Revision questions on Chapters 41–52

1 Do you think that the deaths of Mr Hale and Mr Bell are adequately prepared for? Give reasons for your answer.

2 Before his death, what influence does Mr Bell have on the action?

3 Describe Margaret's reactions to Helstone on her visit revisiting it with Mr Bell.

4 What indications are there that Margaret is really in love with Thornton before she admits to it? Refer closely to the text.

5 Write an essay in appreciation of Mrs Gaskell's irony at the expense of the Harley Street set.

6 Do you find the ending of the novel realistic or contrived? Give reasons for your answer.

Mrs Gaskell's Art in *North and South*
The characters

Margaret Hale

her superb ways of moving and looking . . . full of a soft feminine defiance . . .
her round white flexile throat rising out of the full, yet lithe figure . . . her eyes,
with their soft gloom . . .

It is little wonder that for some time Mrs Gaskell thought of calling
her novel *Margaret Hale*, for Margaret is the central character and
most of the events of the novel are seen through her eyes. Our first
introduction to her in the back drawing-room at Harley Street
sufficiently indicates her capacity for service to others. She is socially
subordinate to Edith yet secretly delighting in her dreams of
Helstone. Already we begin to wonder a little at her situation, the
holidays always in Harley Street, Edith's obvious dependence on her,
and her own dissonance from this kind of superficial society, which is
to be so mercilessly pilloried by Mrs Gaskell at the beginning and the
end of her novel. Much of Margaret is explained by retrospect, that
established way of providing psychological integration of character.
Her loneliness; the sense of isolation; the ability to withdraw into
herself (she lies quietly 'for fear of making her father unhappy by her
grief'); a sense of ingratitude – all these show that Margaret the child
is mother to Margaret the woman. All is not lost, and the grown-up
Margaret knows that her room in Harley Street has special memories
for her that give her a sense of regret. Even here her independence of
spirit is evident, for she is critical of the trifles that constitute so much
of the preparation for Edith's marriage.

Margaret has a strong attachment to Helstone, but her life is beset
by burdens. The first (referred to in the text, Chapter 2) is the scant
detail on Frederick, but when she reaches Helstone with her father we
are given an account of her which is strongly individualized, sexual,
and anything but directly conventional. We are told that she delighted in 'crushing down the fern with a cruel glee, as she felt it yield
under her light foot'. But there is also a tendency to idealize (or perhaps idyllize) the place possessively, so that 'She took a pride in her
forest. Its people were her people.' Set against the happy return is the
obvious moodiness and abstraction of her father, and her mother's
constitutional dislike of the place – she cannot stand living in the

neighbourhood of so many trees. Margaret herself is happiest out of doors. She rather resents the fact that Dixon is her mother's confidante; she feels that secrets (about Frederick) are being withheld from her and, with the arrival of Henry Lennox, another kind of pressure is put upon her.

Lennox's proposal to her and Margaret's reception of it are crucial to our understanding of her character. Before the proposal she is innocence personified; during it she is startled into unpleasant reality. Afterwards, 'She was grave, and little disposed to speak', and as she broods on Lennox after his departure she is unhappy, and almost wishes she could have loved him. Margaret has a strong sense of conscience, and this means that she examines what she does and says and often finds herself wanting. But outwardly she conveys pride and, sometimes, disdain. She has responsibility thrust upon her. She has to deal with her father's leaving the church; she has to break that news to her mother; she has to tell her of the impending move; she has to make all practical arrangements for the move. Margaret is religious in the sense that she rests heavily on her faith in crisis, and we cannot overestimate the effect that Mr Hale's giving up the ministry has on her. She regards her father as 'a schismatic – an outcast'. And while she is trying to cope with her parents' interaction she has also to cope with Dixon's reactions. She is forced to put her in her place; and afterwards we are told, Dixon never ceased to admire her. It is typical of Margaret that she insists they retain Dixon when they move.

Margaret is nostalgic. When she leaves Helstone she takes a last walk, even idealizing the lives of the poachers she hears. But when she arrives in Milton she manages to convey her inner strength; in her first greeting of Thornton she shows no awkwardness, 'but she seemed to assume some kind of rule over him at once.' Margaret in fact seems to Thornton to be haughty, but we should beware of placing too much value on this subjective judgement. What we should note is Margaret's inherent snobbery; although she senses Thornton's power and resolution, she speaks of him as being 'not quite a gentleman, but that was hardly to be expected.' Margaret is an unusual heroine in that she is not always a sympathetic one; the reader is irritated by her assumption of superiority (we feel with Thornton) and at times by her bloody-mindedness. But she is not yet twenty when she has to assume so much because of the weakness of her parents. Some of her standards are those of what her mother would call a lady: she has taste and abhors vulgarity. Mrs Gaskell is, however, showing character in action, and Margaret learns much; has to adapt herself; and ultimately comes to recognize that she isn't quite what she thought herself to be.

Margaret begins to live in the streets of Milton. That is, she comes up against the common people, and has 'to endure undisguised admiration from these outspoken men.' It is the beginning of her education, a long cry from Harley Street. More directly it brings her into sympathetic contact with the Higginses through her spontaneous giving of the flowers. As Mrs Gaskell puts it, 'she had found a human interest.' This, which I am sure her author would call practical Christianity, is Margaret's salvation. Because of this she gains the strength to deal with the successive domestic crises thrust upon her; more importantly, it makes her question the relationship of masters and men, and it brings her finally to a true appraisal of Thornton.

Margaret's pride, however, shows itself early on to Thornton, by whom she is irritated (she hands him his cup of tea 'with the proud air of an unwilling slave'). But she is a little susceptible (she would never admit it) and admires the rareness of Thornton's smile. Indeed, she is so susceptible that she becomes impassioned in defence of her beloved South. Her argument with Thornton shows her obduracy and bias but, and this is typical of Margaret, when she withholds a handshake she immediately regrets it. Even in these 'First Impressions' she is beginning to shift her ground from rooted snobbery, saying of Thornton that 'his statement of having been a shop-boy was the thing I like best of all.' She detests the measuring of everything by the standard of wealth, but when Mrs Thornton and Fanny visit her she shows sensitivity in feeling that Fanny should take an interest in the 'manufactories' that provide her wealth. She is still storing up her memories of Helstone, and confides them to Bessy. Her frankness impresses Mrs Thornton but she soon destroys any passing good impression she has created in that proud and stern lady by making it sarcastically clear that she has no designs on her son. With that son she is in open conflict, stressing human rights, mutual dependence and 'that spirit which suffereth long, and is kind, and seeketh not her own.'

One of Margaret's major attributes, her moral courage, is seen in her facing up to great adversity. Dr Donaldson is impressed by her response to the news of her mother's terminal illness. She suffers deeply ('How shall I bear it?') but has to conceal the situation from her father, handle Dixon, visit Bessy. She lies to her father, saying that her mother is not seriously ill; she goes to the Thorntons with him, 'her heart heavy with various anxieties', joins in the conversation and returns home to find her mother barely alive. She then has to endure her father's recriminations. Her next visit to the Thorntons is the climacteric one. Here her courage, her sense of justice, in short her humanity, are strikingly in evidence. She appeals to Thornton, 'Save these poor strangers whom you have decoyed here', and when she realizes she has driven him closer to a terrible confrontation she spares nothing to protect him. The result is humiliation for her as she hears the gossip about herself and Thornton. With great courage she goes home despite her injuries, and keeps back from her parents what she has done. We should note the consistency of her actions; she is brave and impetuous at one and the same time.

Such is her shame about the gossip that when she faces Thornton the next day she does him less than justice – 'Your way of speaking shocks me. It is blasphemous . . . your whole manner offends me' – yet Thornton is paying her the great compliment of loving her. It is this kind of limitation in Margaret that humanizes her; we realize that she is not yet mature enough to know that gossip is of little consequence when compared with reality. And in her fear she goes to extremes, telling Thornton that she had more feeling for all the men in that desperate crowd than she had for him. I suggest that this is spite born of misguided pride and fear, and that because she has been humiliated she seeks to humiliate Thornton in his turn. Admittedly, she refers to Thornton's kindness to her father, but it is too late; although she feels self-reproach at having injured him, she asserts that she would act so again. Mrs Gaskell is here subtle; the fact is that Margaret is suffering so much from a variety of causes that she is near breakdown, and clarity of judgement suffers as a result.

'She disliked him the more for having mastered her inner will.' This is Margaret in reaction after Thornton's proposal, and we are tempted to say that it shows how strongly she is drawn to his strength. She thinks she hates, but the very fact that she is moved indicates Thornton's influence over her. She now has the pressures of her mother's obsession to have Frederick home; she writes to him, but is torn apart by her fear that he will be caught. Next she calls upon her courage again, and goes to see the dead Bessy. The result is a direct crisis: she talks Higgins out of violent recourse to drink, takes him home (how far from Harley Street she has come in her social education). Yet she doesn't hesitate to tell Higgins that the Union is a tyranny because it prescribes their conduct to men. Frederick's arrival is followed almost immediately by Mrs Hale's death, and Margaret has to call up all her reserves of stamina and practical organization to cope with her father and brother. And, most importantly, her faith sustains her.

The saving lie about not being at the railway station does Margaret considerable inward injury, and again I suggest that it shows her subterranean inclination for Thornton. Immediately afterwards she has to support her father (physically and spiritually) at the funeral, and then herself in the face of the inspector's questioning. There is little wonder that she faints when he has left, or that she is deeply shocked when she learns that, on Mr Thornton's instructions, there is to be no inquest. Her main thought is that she 'stood as a liar in his eyes'. As Mrs Gaskell puts it, Margaret cannot acknowledge to herself 'how much she valued his respect and good opinion'. She is well on the way to being in love.

Mrs Gaskell even suggests that this unacknowledged love is based on a kind of sexual fear, on maidenly independence. 'But Mr Thornton – why did she tremble, and hide her face in the pillow? What strong feeling had overtaken her at last?' She is so weakened by the thought (and by her other burdens) that she is very touched by her father's tenderness to her. With Boucher's death she is thrown into practical activity again, but she is still obsessed by Thornton's opinion, remembering his kindness to her mother, and wishing he would come to see them. Instead, his mother comes according to her promise to Mrs Hale, and Margaret experiences further degradation, though she soon realizes that Thornton himself has behaved with delicacy and concern on her account. But when he does speak to her about the incident at the station both her pride and his get in the way of any love and sympathy. Margaret, always human, affects a great deal of merriment she does not feel in order to cover the wound.

Most interesting is Margaret's reaction to the advent of Mr Bell. His wit and his bluntness – particularly with regard to Thornton – call forth a defence of the latter by Margaret which gives Mr Bell an insight into her feelings. With her father's death in Oxford Margaret is prostrated. The arrival of her aunt Shaw, with her likeness to Margaret's dead mother, depresses her but points her in the direction of Harley Street again. It would be true to say that she has little strength for resistance, though she agrees to do what Mr Bell suggests, and also insists on visiting Mrs Thornton and Higgins. In a strange way this shows where her sympathies lie. When she says goodbye to Thornton, after having stood on the spot where she had tried to protect him, she offers him her handshake, and he lets go of it 'as carelessly as if it had been a dead and withered flower'. It is this, plus her emotional exhaustion, that makes Margaret anxious to get away from Milton. She is divided against herself; one of the last currents of feeling causes her to give her father's Bible to Higgins.

Yet in Harley Street she even frets for the small house in Milton. She longs for Dixon to bring her news of the place. She longs for Mr Bell to put things right for her with Mr Thornton. When Mr Bell suggests a visit to Helstone, she longs to go. When they arrive, she begins the final stage in the education of her feelings. It is a salutary one. There is the felling of the trees; the roasting of the cat; the changed schoolroom and the changed methods; there is the changed Vicarage. Above all, there is the changed Margaret. She has been living in a world of suffering reality, not one of 'adjective absolutes'. Her three years' absence has wrought changes that go beyond knowledge to self-knowledge. It is superbly put by Mrs Gaskell:

A sense of change, of individual nothingness, of perplexity and disappointment, overpowered Margaret. Nothing had been the same; and this slight, all-pervading instability, had given her greater pain than if all had been too entirely changed for her to recognize it.

Soon she has 'a strange undefined longing' to hear that Mr Bell has seen Mr Thornton; it is the index to her feelings. She releases these in her 'sweetest moments' with Edith's small son. She becomes aware too of Henry Lennox's interest in her, and perhaps directly aware of the differences between them. With the death of Mr Bell, Margaret cries over 'this fatal year'. But she finds the core of integrity that has guided her through life (despite her 'lies') and she prays 'that she might have strength to speak and act the truth for evermore'.

Her hours by the seaside give her, with her perspective, a sense of direction, a framework within which she may act. Henry Lennox becomes the advocate of Milton without knowing that he will effect his own failure. Once Margaret sees Thornton (she hasn't done so for more than a year) she finds herself watching his face, listening for his voice and, when he tells her of the round-robin from the men, 'looking straight into his face with her speaking eyes.' Her actions are even more eloquent. To use a colloquial phrase, she now makes the running; Margaret has found her heart (and Lennox's absence shows that he knows what she feels), but such is her nature that she cannot reveal it except in this oblique way. Her words 'Oh, Mr Thornton, I am not good enough!' show how far she has come. A few moments later 'She slowly faced him, glowing with beautiful shame.' Both reactions are a measure of her own passionate nature and of scarce-understood sexual awakening. Her last words show, too, a sense of humour that bodes well for her future relationship with her mother-in-law.

Mr Hale

The face was in repose; but it was rather rest after weariness, than the serene calm of the countenance of one who led a placid, contented life.

Mr Hale's biographical derivations seem to come from Mrs Gaskell's father, who renounced the ministry, and from her husband, who often opted out of domestic crises involving the children. Mr Hale is a subtle piece of characterization, mainly because of his combination of weakness and an odd kind of strength. He is indecisive yet makes the one decision that changes his life and that of his family. His reasons for leaving the church are not sufficiently clarified to be really convincing, but everything else about him is consistent. He suffers under the intolerable burden of having married a Miss Beresford whose social – or perhaps society – ideas were ill-suited to her being the wife of a poor clergyman. And this is where Mrs Gaskell's subtlety comes in. Mrs Hale is envied because of the bright, sensitive, handsome man she marries; but romance is not reality, and Mr Hale proves to be a man who cannot adjust to the rough buffetings of the world. He is a good man, who goes about his Christian business in the neighbourhood. But his wife is a hypochondriac (the terrible irony is that she comes to be really ill) who subjects him to the permanent blackmail of complaint – about Helstone and the number of trees, for example, which oppress her and cause her to be as she is. Mr Hale's is a divided marriage – not that he would admit this – since Dixon is more properly his wife's companion than he is. His decision has to be conveyed via Margaret; he is unequal to the occasion himself. Impractical, he relies on Margaret to do this and to organize the move. The breaking-point in his life is the breaking of Frederick through the mutiny; his major fear is that Frederick will be executed, and this is the burden he bears. His real tragedy, however, is the knowledge that he cannot *share* the burden with his wife. She too is unequal to pressure.

Mr Hale's career in Milton-Northern is an unlikely one, but he manages to survive. He likes and respects Thornton; he treats Higgins with natural courtesy, which wins over that gruff and sometimes aggressive character. He is incapable of dealing with the crisis of Boucher's death, which devolves upon Margaret; he cannot be told of his wife's illness because of the strain it would put him under, but when she dies he is prostrated. When he and Margaret arrive home after the Thornton dinner-party, Mrs Gaskell tells us that he became an old man in a matter of minutes. Yet though he depends on Margaret he shows her great tenderness when she is emotionally exhausted by the series of deaths and the inner frustrations of feeling herself degraded in Thornton's eyes. His death, like that of Mr Bell, comes as something of a surprise. Perhaps it shouldn't, since he has a frailty of spirit that anyway makes his survival in life tenuous.

Mrs Hale

'Married for love, what can dearest Maria have to wish for in this world?'

Mrs Hale never forgets the social position she might, indeed ought to have had. She would dearly have liked to appear at Edith's wedding provided that she had (a) the good health to do so and (b) the fashionable clothes she regards as essential. Tender and kind to Margaret, she is always urging her husband to seek preferment so that she can recapture her position in society. Her illness appears to be simulated because of her dissatisfactions, but it comes to have a terrible actuality. She reproaches her husband for not telling her of their move, she is in any case oppressed by Helstone; she panics, or is ashamed, or is incapable of coping (or all three) when Henry Lennox turns up unexpectedly for lunch. Her conscious role of invalid is, one feels, aided and abetted by Dixon. But Mrs Hale is tenacious of purpose: she never lets Mr Hale forget that she is ill (and there is an innuendo in their marriage that makes him feel he is responsible). She never settles in Milton-Northern, but her tenacity, a kind of courage and tenderness, is shown in her asking Mrs Thornton to visit her. Before that, she has requested Dr Donaldson that Margaret be kept ignorant of the true state of her health. But Margaret has her mother's tenacity and approaches the susceptible Dr Donaldson directly. Mrs Hale's scene with Mrs Thornton is one of the finest in the novel. The dying woman does not get exactly what she wants from the 'ungraciously truthful' and unyielding mother, but she gets enough to satisfy her of the sincerity of what is promised.

Mrs Hale also proves tenacious in a related situation. Knowing that her husband lacks the nerve to write to Frederick, she persuades Margaret to do so. There is an element of emotional blackmail about this, and even if we allow for the strength of a mother's love, there is a degree of selfishness in her risking Frederick's life. Having said that, let us admit the naturalness of her pressure on Margaret. In presenting the Hales' marriage as she does, Mrs Gaskell is spelling out the bases of what today would be called incompatibility. That Mr Hale loves his wife there is little doubt; that she loved him but has grown to love herself better in her invalidism is equally certain. Mrs Hale's psychology is finely exposed, with the masterly irony of her being terminally ill having a moving and fatalistic quality.

Frederick Hale

His eyes were generally merry-looking, but at times they and his mouth so suddenly changed, and gave her such an idea of latent passion, that it almost made her afraid.

The above quotation is only part of the story, but that story is in commentary rather than fact. Frederick cannot come alive as a character – there isn't time for him to develop – mainly because he exists as a symbol of righteous rebellion, whose life has been changed by impetuosity and a sense of moral justice. Now it can be argued that Margaret is impetuous (her mother is too, hence the wish to see Mrs Thornton) and that she has a sense of moral justice, so much so that she finally changes her bias. Frederick is therefore given a family consistency, but it is only an outline. In fact the truest facet of Frederick's character is, I suggest, his adaptable selfishness, which enables him to stop fighting for justice and marry the available, well-off Roman Catholic Dolores Barbour. There is no time for Mrs Gaskell to develop Frederick. He refers to his father's leaving Helstone as a blunder, walks about as if he is on a quarter-deck, and speaks thus to Margaret:

'poor little woman! what! is this face all wet with tears? I will hope. I will, in spite of a thousand doctors. Bear up, Margaret, and be brave enough to hope!' (Chapter 30)

But Frederick is his father's son. In crisis or adversity his inherited weakness is seen: 'For Frederick had broken down now, and all his theories were of no use to him.' (Chapter 30) He soon gets over this grief, concentrates (through Margaret) on the practicality of getting away, behaves like a man of action in pushing Leonards, shows some interest in Lennox's taking up his case but (rather like his mother) settles naturally into doing what he wants to do. He marries and settles in Cadiz, becomes a Roman Catholic and is undoubtedly prosperous.

Mr Thornton

'About thirty – with a face that is neither exactly plain, nor yet handsome, nothing remarkable – not quite a gentleman; but that was hardly to be expected.'

The above quotation is given here because of the discussion of the terms 'man' and 'gentleman' between Thornton and Margaret. By his own standards he is a man, and by any standards a man respected among men. For the most part we see him in constant interaction with Margaret, or Mr Hale, or his mother or, later, Higgins. In the last phase of the novel he is seen mixing with those who respect his abilities.

Thornton is a man of strong principle and strong passion. He must be doing something. When he first meets Margaret he is irritated at being kept waiting – until he sees her. Then he is irritated – but strongly attracted – by her assumption of authority. He is impetuous, reacting strongly (perhaps over-reacting) to imagined slights or differences of mood. Thus when Margaret does not shake hands with him when he leaves he is offended. He always speaks strongly, even to his mother when she taxes him with being caught by a penniless girl. But perhaps his most marked characteristic is his pride, and this is in evidence on a number of occasions, more particularly when Margaret urges him to face the men and save his Irish labourers. His pride is well to the fore when Margaret expresses herself offended by his proposal. Allied to his pride is his passion; he shows a strong sexual awareness of Margaret from the very beginning of his acquaintance with her. We remember particularly his watching the movements of the bracelet, her pushing it until 'it tightened her soft flesh'. John Thornton is susceptible and falls in love. And having fallen, he remains true in feeling and in fact to the woman who has thus moved him.

He is a man of his time, strongly biased in favour of employer power and exulting in it. This gives him a kind of arrogance, though in fact the authoritarian bark is worse than his practical bite. The fact that he has made his own way despite the adversity thrust upon the family by his father is sufficient indication of his iron will. He considers Margaret proud and disagreeable – at least, he thinks he does! Strange, therefore, that he should wish his mother and sister to call on them, and that he should be so peremptory in his insistence on Fanny's going. Yet he is considerate and generous in some ways – remember his bringing the doctor's address to Margaret and the baskets of fruit for Mrs Hale. But he cannot help antagonizing Margaret or she him, for his creed is measured over and above what she calls the human right: it is quite unequivocally, 'We, the owners of capital, have a right to choose what we will do with it.' It is to Thornton's great credit that he moves away from the obduracy of this position and that the men who work for him, notably Higgins, respect him for his positive employment of human rights.

His intense practicality and capacity for organization are seen on the eve of the strike and riot. His discussion with Margaret finds him saying, 'A man is to me a higher and a completer being than a gentleman.' He is uncompromisingly assertive; his toughness is wittily put by Margaret: 'He is my first olive: let me make a face while I swallow it.' Margaret calls his courage in question but she has no need to do so. He even provokes the storm that floods round him. With Margaret injured he is himself wounded to the emotional heart, and utters his love to her senseless form. Once committed, he is always committed: he braves his mother's remonstrances and proposes to the weary, embattled Margaret. Her rejection wounds him even more deeply, but he responds with purposeful dignity. When he leaves, Margaret 'thought she had seen the gleam of unshed tears in his eyes'. For much of the rest of the day he is 'almost blinded by his baffled passion'. He is so broken that he goes back to his mother and tells her that she is the only one who loves him. He cannot help loving Margaret all the more. And he does what so many do in this kind of suffering: he throws himself into practical activity. He does not succeed in distancing himself from his emotions.

By throwing himself into his interests and theirs he commands the respect of his fellow employers. Mrs Gaskell observes 'He felt his power and revelled in it,' yet there is little of arrogance in what he does. With his realization of Mrs Hale's illness he shows a true generosity of spirit, though we are told that he 'had no general benevolence'. When he delivers the fruit he apologizes for 'rough ways – too abrupt I fear', for this is the mark of inferiority that Margaret has unwittingly put upon him. The mark becomes as painful as a bruise when he sees Margaret at the station with the unknown man. But his sense of right conduct leads him to inquire after her, though he finds it difficult to 'galvanize his trust' in Margaret's integrity. He comes near to hate, but in a fine image Mrs Gaskell defines the unrelenting nature of his fascination: 'He was in the Charybdis of passion, and must perforce circle and circle ever nearer round the fatal centre.'

Thornton's sympathy, particularly towards her father, moves

Margaret, but after he has seen the police-inspector he is faced with a difficult decision. He decides to protect the woman he loves; he orders that there shall be no inquest. In effect he has committed moral perjury, structurally a neatly balancing corollary to Margaret's saving lie that has put him in this position. And all the while the fierce agony of his jealousy continues: he is irritable, angry with his mother for suggesting that Margaret has a lover, yet supposing the truth of it himself. Still his nobler feelings triumph over his emotional, and even physical, suffering. His main reason in getting his mother to visit Margaret is because he feels that she is 'in some strait and difficulty connected with an attachment which, of itself from my knowledge of Miss Hale's character, is perfectly innocent and right.' There speaks the deep truth of the man but, as in so many of us, it is overturned by feelings that tell him a different story.

It is at this time, when he is beset by worries about his capital, order, and the self-imposed nemesis of his incompetent Irish labourers, that he is approached by Higgins. When he hears who he is, Thornton employs his own sarcasm ('You don't want impudence') to lacerate him but – and this is typical of Thornton – he ponders on the fact that Higgins has waited five hours to see him. He calls on Higgins and apologizes, though he is disconcerted by the initial presence of Margaret, and tells her later with ill-constrained brusqueness that her secret is safe with him and that his passion for her is over. It manifestly isn't, and when Mr Bell arrives he considers that Thornton is 'terribly gone off both in intelligence and manner'. In conversation Thornton asks bitterly if Margaret is '*so* remarkable for truth' but, again typically, 'could have bitten his tongue out' for his passionate impetuosity. Mr Bell, of course, sees into the heart of the matter. Thornton shows a 'trembling interest' when he learns that Margaret is going to live in Harley Street.

The extent of her influence is such that, despite his own tenuous financial position, he is flexible enough to establish what is properly a works canteen in Marlborough Mills. He is practical enough too to see that the workmen pay him a rent for it. When Margaret does go he behaves with a lack of grace despite the associations of where they are – on the spot where she tried to protect him. Soon 'His pride in the commercial character he had established for himself' is put to the severest test, but he has the consolation – and he appreciates it – of knowing that Margaret has no lover; that it was Frederick he saw. In giving up his business he has the satisfaction (it helps his pride) of paying off all he owes. He also acquires a new humility, born not of shame but out of the simplicity, care and struggles of the past. We may say, too, that his love for Margaret has helped him to come to terms with his situation. He refuses to enter into a dubious speculation because of his responsibilities to others. His integrity is upheld in this final adversity which, as he will come to see, has its particular sweet uses. His honesty – Henry Lennox tries to save him from it – wins him the respect of Colthurst. He takes more pride, one feels, in the round-robin than in anything else; he may have failed in terms of economics, but he has succeeded positively in the 'human right'. His sudden coming together with Margaret, his recognition of what she is doing for him *because* she loves him, sees the resurgence of the passion he has always felt for her. In the final analysis he is a 'man' by his own definition: physical, compelling, positive, learning, losing, but winning the only thing that matters, the love that has not changed despite all the changes of circumstance. He is a masterly psychological portrait, wonderfully consistent, a kind of industrial Darcy with a more direct sexual magnetism.

Mrs Thornton

The firm, severe, dignified woman, who never gave way in street courtesy, or paused in her straight-onward course to the clearly-defined end which she proposed to herself.

Mrs Thornton is recognizably like her son – one of Mrs Gaskell's great strengths is her ability to convey family similarities – for she is strong and has had to overcome poverty and privation. In practice she is harder than he is, though she does soften on the occasion when she goes to see Mrs Hale and realizes that she is much more ill than she had thought. She has certain affiliations, though greater inflexibility, with Mrs Morel in D. H. Lawrence's *Sons and Lovers*, where the possessive love of the mother prevents the son from having a full relationship with another woman. But though Mrs Thornton is depicted as jealous and though she feels that Margaret is out to trap her son into marriage, she is also shown as virtually without sexuality. Presumably it was withered by contact with the dissolute husband responsible for their family deprivations. All her love, passionate love in the possessive sense, has been re-invested in her son, though her 'pitying tenderness of manner' to her daughter covers an affection that is protective and intent on conquering her daughter's weakness. Like her son, she is proud, referring to Margaret as 'a penniless girl', 'a renegade clergyman's daughter' who has no right to turn up her nose at her son. Like him, she is passionate and impetuous, saying almost in the same breath 'I hate her!'

Mrs Thornton puts John before everything; we are told that 'she walked proudly among women for his sake.' She is shy, since it is only since her son's prosperity that she has been free to go into society. She is fond of Milton and says so. She is biased and unfair in her judgement of Margaret, telling Fanny not to make a friend of her because 'She will do you no good.' In her own way she is an inverted snob, rejecting her son's study of the classics when he should be giving all his time and attention to maintaining his position. She soon reveals that she has an exaggerated pride in her son's position in Milton – and further afield – as a manufacturer. But she respects Margaret's frankness, and 'smiled a grim smile' when she responds to it. She is not so pleased by Margaret's considering it ludicrous that she might be suspected of setting her cap at Thornton. There are moments during this early conversation when she seems to be testing Margaret, the 'If you live in Milton, you must learn to have a brave heart,' being unconsciously ironic in view of the fact that Margaret is so courageous when the riot actually occurs.

She befriends (her word) Margaret at her son's request. At the riot she is at one stage 'white with fear' as she sees the faces of the mob, but she does not forget Margaret, tells her she will have to bear what they have to bear, and insists on staying with her son. Her fingers tremble, there is terror in her voice, and she sticks it out. She is alarmed when Margaret is injured, and insists on going for the doctor herself when Jane and her daughter refuse to go. When she returns she is so concerned that she tries to stop Margaret from leaving. But afterwards she taunts her son – such is her jealousy – for needing to be protected by a girl. She is betraying her fears, and these become overt when he tells her that he must propose to Margaret. With admirable self-control Mrs Thornton crushes down 'her own personal mortification' when her son fails to notice an expression of maternal feelings. She has her triumph however, telling Thornton after his rejection that 'Mother's love is given by God, John. It holds fast for ever and ever. A girl's love is like a puff of smoke – it changes with every wind.' (Chapter 26). She then shows her teeth like a dog. The image would suggest that Mrs Gaskell is exaggerating, but we do not doubt it.

Her visit to Mrs Hale emphasizes the contrast between the two women, but it also contains a remarkable insight into the outwardly repressed exterior of Mrs Thornton. She responds to Mrs Hale because she remembers a daughter of her own who had died in infancy. The softening is hardly apparent; she merely indicates 'with grave severity' that she will keep her word. It is characteristic of Mrs Thornton's stern nature that she adds her own rider to the request – that is a determination to tell Margaret 'faithfully and plainly' if she ever finds her doing wrong. She is 'ungraciously truthful' to the last.

We cannot help feeling that Mrs Thornton rather enjoys telling her son that it was the man with Margaret who gave Leonards the push (although he already knows this). He asks her to see Margaret, urging her to show 'a merciful judgment for Margaret's indiscretion'. He does not know his mother. She feels bitterness and hate, 'snorted scornfully over the picture of the beauty of her victim', and spends half the night preparing how best to devastate Margaret. She succeeds, but perhaps not as directly as she had hoped. Margaret has spirit, dignity, concealed tears, and finally disdain, which leaves Mrs Thornton in possession of the field but hardly with complete victory. We are told that she is somewhat mollified by Margaret's passion. After the deaths of her parents, Margaret is further accused by Mrs Thornton of being weak: she echoes Mr Bell's words that Margaret is a lap-dog to her Harley Street relatives, who are anyway somewhat late in appearing. She disapproves of John's setting up a works canteen, but when Margaret comes to say goodbye she is sufficiently moved by her to say that she believes that her conduct was not unbecoming. This is a big concession, almost as if she has read intuitively that her son will go on loving Margaret and that she may one day stand in a closer relationship to her. We are not sure that she feels this; merely that she senses the imperishable nature of her son's love.

Mrs Thornton succeeds in putting down Mrs Shaw with admirable bluntness. Her last scene is, appropriately, with the son she loves. She has spent the anxious nights as he works on his calculations, just as sleeplessly as he has. When he tells her that he has failed, she is so moved that she almost pushes the idea of the speculation to him. She speaks with 'gloomy defiance' and wonders 'where justice was gone to' that a man of his character and ability can fail. When he begs her to help by recalling the simplicity of childhood in prayer and piety, she responds by saying that God has 'seen fit to be very hard on you, very.' In the final instance, though, this extraordinary woman, whose will has helped to fashion his, realizes that she has the one great blessing of having him alive. In a compelling sense, we feel that Mrs Thornton is better in adversity than in happiness. She was born for severity, gloom, opposition, denial; her pride vested in an abiding sense of duty

– not unlike a Roman matron joying in her husband's warrior prowess.

Fanny Thornton

'I have a headache today . . .'

Fanny is spoiled and weak, and we need give her little space here. She suffers from imaginary ailments, is indolent, dislikes Milton and the way of life there, and has the simple ambition to go to London and to the Alhambra. She has to make do with Mr Watson (there is considerable irony employed by Mrs Gaskell on the wedding preparations, which complement Edith's) whose speculations make them rich. Fanny will have her carriages, and will be sufficiently removed from anything like the strike-riot she endured. Her lack of courage is meant to contrast with Margaret's spirit. Mrs Thornton's shame on her account is such that she covers it by terms of endearment. Mrs Gaskell is here not concerned with family likeness so much as the fact that Fanny was too young to know suffering and has only known the degrees of affluence. Thornton himself reprimands her on one occasion, but overspends on her wedding. This too may be a compensation for her lack of character.

Nicholas Higgins

a poorly-dressed, middle-aged workman . . . This man looked so careworn.

Nicholas is indeed bowed but not broken by care. Apart from the strong individuality of his character, he has an important functional role in the plot – it is through him that Margaret comes to a full appraisal of the industrial situation in Milton-Northern and of the divisions between masters and men. It is also through Higgins that Thornton comes to an appraisal of (a) the individual qualities of his workmen (he marvels at and is perhaps made to feel guilty by Higgins's long wait for him) and (b) the working partnership possible between masters and men, seen in Thornton's renting the men a works' canteen. At first we feel very sorry for Higgins, mainly because of the fact that Bessy is dying. Yet despite this there is a directness in his judgement that is winning; he epitomizes Mrs Gaskell's major theme of reconciliation when he says 'yo' see North and South has both met and made kind o' friends in this big smoky place.' (Chapter 8). He is sturdily independent, a little gruff and suspicious, not liking strange folk in his own house. Bessy tells Margaret that Nicholas is 'vexed and put about' because she didn't keep her promise to call. He is gruff, as Bessy predicted he would be when he sees Margaret, resents her preaching to Bessy, and roundly asserts 'I believe what I see, and no more.' At the same time he is so grateful for Margaret's kindness to Bessy that he says he wishes there were a God so that he could ask him to bless Margaret.

Higgins defines the nature of the strike for Margaret and also reveals his bias against the soft South, saying that down there they have too little spirit to strike. Nicholas and his union are resisting the taking of less money than they had earned before. Where he is wrong is in saying that the state-of-trade argument is 'a piece of masters' humbug'. He also gives Margaret some insight into Thornton as employer by referring to him as an 'oud bulldog'. He is determined to fight, and when he learns that Margaret is going to the Thorntons for dinner he breaks out, saying how much he wishes he could get to talk to the bosses. He goes for Boucher for his lack of spirit, yet we know that he feels compassion for the family and, later, he is to show it in a particularly self-denying way. Although he later re-thinks his position, Nicholas early in the strike asserts 'there's no help for us but having faith i' th' Union. They'll win the day, see if they dunnot!' The terrible reality Nicholas soon has to face is that they 'dunnot'.

Nicholas abhors the violence that ruins the men's case. He even threatens to tell the police where they can find those who orchestrated the riot. But with the death of Bessy he is shattered in another way. His threat of violence and drink, his breaking down, his listening to Margaret and then going with her to see her father, all this is told with a graphic intensity. Higgins, like the important characters in this major novel, undergoes change; on a simple level, his feeling that he should have cleaned himself before going to the Hales shows an awareness outside the narrow confines of self. He gradually articulates a simple belief – largely because Bessy has lived by and for her faith – and he also articulates the power of the unions, which send people to Coventry if they don't conform. He adheres to his daily faith as Margaret adheres to her spiritual one. 'Our only chance is binding men together in one common interest.' He little knows when he says this that he is to be instrumental in achieving just that by working with and for Thornton.

Higgins has a hard time getting work – 'Sorrows is more plentiful than dinners just now' – with the employers able to eliminate those men who supported the Union so strongly. He draws an analogy between the Union and a plough that is preparing the harvest, but he is 'welly felled' when he sees Boucher's body. He can't face Mrs Boucher. He has to be left alone, but then determines to support the family because of the moral responsibility he owes them. He seems to feel that he has driven Boucher to his death. He has too much pride to sign Hamper's pledge and even thinks of going south to get work.

Perhaps we have some doubts about Higgins's capacity for change. His rebuttal by Thornton shows him to be a man of spirit and stamina, but even better is his acceptance of employment by Thornton, when he has the nerve – and honesty – to suggest that he and Thornton deserve each other. They do, but each shifts a little, with Higgins almost coming to admire the bulldog who is at least open. It is a tribute to his sincerity that Margaret should give him her father's Bible, but he remains a functional character to the end. It is Higgins who finally enlightens Thornton about the presence of Frederick. It is Higgins who helps initiate the works canteen; and it is Higgins who sends the round-robin that helps Thornton to appreciate with pride the 'human right'.

Other characters

Some of these are important in the structure of the novel, while others have the functional impact or stress that we have just noted in Nicholas Higgins. *Bessy* exists as effective contrast to Margaret; brought up in industrial Milton-Northern, knowing no other life, gradually worn down by the ill-health of the wasting disease that kills her. She is the same age as Margaret and a profoundly sympathetic character. She is, like Margaret, religious, but lives almost exclusively for the after-life, the heaven to which she is going after the hell she has found on earth. She gives Margaret a number of insights, first into the industrial life she has experienced at first-hand in the machine room, where the fluff has got into her lungs. She even puts the extreme of the case – that attempts to improve working conditions have been opposed by some workers because the fluff itself was regarded as substitute food. Bessy recognizes the essential goodness in Margaret and, despite her suffering, always greets her with a loving affection. She is concerned for her father but very fair, indicating that he drinks but rarely and that he is her support and stay. There is little doubt that Bessy is a symbol of suffering and genuine faith, but she also has a keen intelligence and awareness of the current strike situation which she is able to convey to Margaret.

Mary has none of Bessy's ill-health but, as far as we can see, none of her intelligence or faith either. She is functional in that she helps Dixon, and of course is roundly told off by that exacting lady, but it is interesting that she is used by her father as an expression of his gratitude and pride. He will not accept payment from Margaret or Mr Hale for her services.

Dixon is a remarkable creation, one of Mrs Gaskell's servant galaxy: vivid, immediate, racy in speech; devoted to Mrs Hale and almost jealously protective of her; still after all these years a little resentful of Mr Hale, and still considering him not quite good enough for the Miss Beresford he was lucky enough to marry. Her first outburst is typical: 'And master thinking of turning Dissenter at his time of life'. She causes Margaret to respond in a very positive way; she puts Dixon, so to speak, in her downstairs place. The result is that Dixon respects Margaret all the more, and tells herself that she has 'a touch of the old gentleman about her'. Outwardly she shows that she is prepared to toe the new domestic line by asking Margaret if she may unfasten her gown and do her hair.

In Mr Hale's weak mind there is some doubt as to whether Dixon should accompany them to Milton. Margaret, who is practical, knows how essential Dixon is to her mother. In a sense she is a living reminder of the best of old times. Dixon never loses her prejudice against Mr Hale, and one is forced to admit that there is some justification for it. She cannot help having the occasional snipe, telling him, of Mrs Hale's state before the move, 'The illness seems so much more on the mind than on the body.' Her power makes it virtually impossible to find a girl who could help her, and she complains bitterly about the would-be servants.

Her loyalty is unquestionable. She idolizes Frederick, since he has the breeding she associates with Sir John Beresford. She feels that Margaret may shrink from her mother if she knows the true extent of her illness. Although Margaret rejects this, she knows that they must depend on Dixon, who fears that she will tell her father, 'and a pretty household I shall have of you.' And then, in a remarkable, fluent, emotional and completely caring way she confides in Margaret how much she loves her mother. It is a striking instance of Mrs Gaskell's psychological insight; Dixon never marries, for in a sense Mrs Hale is her family. She nearly breaks down, but reveals after Margaret has kissed her and departed that she loves her too. 'She's as sweet as a nut.' But she continues her recriminations against Mr Hale, saying that he should have made much more of his wife and been more ambitious. We cannot think of the Hales without Dixon. They are her family, and she is part of theirs.

Dixon is a servant snob, worthy to serve her snob mistress. The unwashed Higgins disconcerts her, and, later, Mary is to give her some concern. She thinks of the working classes as servants, and even suggests that she should go to see Bessy laid out. With the prospect of the return of Frederick, Dixon is part of the conspiracy, and comforts Mrs Hale ('we'll keep him snug, depend upon it'), who trusts her. Much of her time is now spent sitting with Mrs Hale while she sleeps. When she dies, Dixon has to quieten Frederick in his excessive sobbing. She urges Margaret not to give way, and then tells her news of the presence of Leonards in the town. She has the good sense not to tell Frederick, and thus plays a functional part in the plot. At the funeral Dixon herself breaks down, but she never tells Margaret of her brief interview with Mr Thornton after the service.

She brings the police-inspector to Margaret, and is obviously upset at having to do so. She notices the strain on Margaret at this time, telling her on one occasion that she is more dead than alive. She cares for Margaret after the death of her father, and clears up the family's affairs in Milton, giving Margaret an account of who bought what at the sale when she returns. She is now Margaret's maid, though Margaret is a little disappointed that she does not say much about the Higginses, Mrs Gaskell explaining that 'Her memory had an aristocratic bias.' She also has, as we might expect, an interest in the fact that Margaret may become Mr Bell's heir, which she would doubtless regard as a happy equivalent to old-time Beresford status. There is a wonderfully humorous exchange between 'old Dixon' and Margaret over the former's curious fear of 'Spain, the Inquisition, and Popish mysteries'. She crosses Edith by putting out the wrong flowers for Margaret's dress, and in this her last appearance is as crotchety and abrasive as ever. She comes alive so vividly in the reader's mind that we cannot help wondering how she will take to Mr Thornton.

Henry Lennox is an outstanding portrayal of the ambitious egoist who knows where he is going. All he needs is the money to get there. His visit to Margaret at Helstone is taken against his sober judgement of waiting, or not even getting involved. Yet Margaret brings out his best side. He realizes that she is different from the Harley Street set – one is tempted to say that he realizes she is real – for although he is part of that set he seems to believe that Margaret would be a permanent advantage to it. His first shock, an important one, is when he realizes that Margaret has been telling only the truth when she referred to the modesty of her father's living. Lennox's ability to be a conversational chameleon is shown in the early charm he exerts over Mr and Mrs Hale, followed by his flippant, cynical sarcasms after his rejection by Margaret. He cannot wait to be away. Clever, and able to contrive sympathy, yet he blunders when it comes to the expression of feelings. His proposal is too abrupt, too sudden for Margaret, and in any case she is innocent in the ways of men of the world. There is little doubt that Lennox is strongly attracted to her sexually, but she is cocooned from such feelings until she meets the compelling conflict of her responses to Thornton. Lennox retires, finally with some grace, from the scene. He is there in the background throughout the attempts to get Frederick off; he is there in the foreground when Margaret returns to Harley Street as a prospective heiress, then a confirmed one. Edith has her little schemes for Henry, who has rather larger schemes of his own. Mrs Gaskell's index to his thoughts and feelings is an unequivocal one:

From this time the clever and ambitious man bent all his powers to gaining Margaret. He loved her sweet beauty. He saw the latent sweep of her mind, which could easily (he thought) be led to embrace all the objects on which he had set his heart. He looked upon her fortune only as a part of the complete and superb character of herself and her position; yet he was fully aware of the rise which it would immediately enable him, the poor barrister, to take. (Chapter 49)

Intimately involved with her business, he has complacent intimations of success. But he goes too far; his condescension over bringing Thornton to the dinner-party blinds him to the impact Thornton had made on Margaret before he was her tenant. His lack of tact, of real sensitivity, had been shown earlier when he had dared to criticize Mr Hale's spiritual decision to Mr Bell, who sees him clearly for what he is – a spurious and superficial conversationalist always with an eye to the main chance. He reaps the whirlwind of failure, and loses Margaret to a man (not a gentleman). But the Henry Lennoxes of this world are survivors, and his suave and unscrupulous nature is bound to succeed.

Edith is spoiled, and the telling comparisons that are drawn with Margaret show her as something of a social parasite. She is fond of Margaret, of that there can be no doubt, but it is a fondness born of need, of having one's caprices indulged. Margaret can model dresses for her and win her little boy out of an obstructive mood; Margaret can act as something of a superior servant to her. Edith simply does not know what life is; what passes for experience is the languid life of

Corfu or the socially acceptable chit-chat of Harley Street, where the numbers at a dinner-party are much more important than any event or individual. She has been over-indulged by her mother; the result is a tinsel glitter and no substance. Her husband is complete caricature; he fits socially, handsomely, dully, indolently and above all romantically into what she needs and what has been determined that she should have. Their's is a romance but not a reality, and it is through such contrasts that Mrs Gaskell makes her moral and social points in *North and South*.

Aunt Shaw is recognizably Edith's mother. Indolent, a society gossip, thinking back to her life and the circumscribed nature of that life with the much older General, she sees in her daughter's marriage a mirror romance of what might have been for her. She is horrified by Milton-Northern, insensitive when she visits Mrs Thornton, intent on dictating to Margaret and ordering her life for her again.

Of the educated characters – using the term in a broad sense – *Mr Bell* stands out. He is all the more remarkable in that he comes into the novel freshly-minted. There is no preparation for him, and no development; Mrs Gaskell conveys him convincingly in his full maturity. His death is sudden, but understandable in view of his eating habits. He is intelligent, witty, with a fund of common sense and a very sharp eye for the details and revelations of other people's lives. He sees into and through Henry Lennox, knowing that this man is on the make. He wonders at the change he notes in Thornton, and then appraises what he calls the *tendresse* between Thornton and Margaret. He knows it exists before Margaret does. He sees that he will not be happy with Mrs Shaw staying in the house in Milton, and moves out.

When he takes Margaret to Helstone he watches her closely – in fact watches *over* her closely – and helps her to register the effects of change. When he comes to Harley Street he not only feels contempt for Lennox but a corresponding ironic displeasure at the fripperies of the ladies. He has a very important function in the plot. Not only does he spell out the financial arrangements for Margaret in Harley Street so that she is *not* bound to stay, he also makes Margaret his heiress and thus enables her to rescue Thornton. His death may therefore be a plot contrivance to effect this. While we want the consummation of Margaret and Thornton (why do we never think of him as John?) we are sad at Mr Bell's departure from the novel.

Other characters are seen merely in passing. Will we ever forget the livid countenance of *Boucher* in the riot, or the determined way in which he drowns himself in a few inches of water? *Mrs Boucher*, too, comes querulously alive, a kind of working-class Mrs Hale who has had to endure terrible privation and poverty, with the children tumbling about her in their filth. There is also the woman who brings the baby for Margaret to place in Mrs Boucher's arms. And, in another class but positively depicted, *Dr Donaldson*, the lifelong bachelor who shows a genuine compassion and a susceptibility to Margaret's charm and beauty.

Mrs Gaskell felt that her novel was hurried too much towards the close of the serial publication. Even with the rewriting and additions, perhaps we should admit that it is one of the weaknesses of *North and South* that the functional relation between character and plot is not always held in balance. Bluntly, there are too many deaths too closely together, and each death releases another character from a kind of bondage; thus Bessy's death releases Higgins to be an active protagonist in the cause of reconciling masters and men; her parents' deaths release Margaret into the world of Mr Bell, of Helstone, of Harley Street; Mr Bell's death releases her from small means to large ones which enable her to marry Thornton and give them both financial independence for life. These points are made solely to indicate functional emphases. In fact Mrs Gaskell maintains a high and integrated level of psychological consistency in her characters.

Settings

Since Mrs Gaskell makes such effective use of contrast in *North and South*, the settings, which provide the basic framework of contrast, must be looked at closely. We are not here concerned to establish the exact proportion of writing space that each location occupies, although in the structure of the novel it is important to note that Milton-Northern occupies the greatest space since it is central to the development of the two main characters. It also embodies the theme, mainly that of the conflict between masters and men. It would be true to say that in *North and South* setting *is* structure, since contrast, conflict and, ultimately, reconciliation, are Mrs Gaskell's intention through her use of specific location.

We begin and end in Harley Street, and it provides the setting for Margaret's somewhat muted early life and the triumph (she would not use the word) of her maturity. Life in Harley Street is governed by society rules – by fashion, by talk, by dinners, by the latest review, by visiting, by the whole paraphernalia of indolence that passes for living. Two outsiders, Mr Bell and Mr Thornton, enter it; Mr Bell refuses to be swallowed and opts out, one taste of Henry Lennox being enough for his finer sensibilities. Mr Thornton virtually swallows it because of his signal integrity. The social range of Harley Street is considerable, but of course there is no one from the working or lower middle class who could be invited. The range embraces the upper-middle class (*North and South* has been called a middle class romance) and some society – Captain Lennox, Henry (a lawyer), magnates, industrialists, commercial men, politicians. They are on display, and they typify that part of the South where money – and some power – lies.

Throughout Mrs Gaskell treats the Shaws and the Lennoxes with quiet irony, yet there is little doubting the needs of Mrs Shaw and their kindness to Margaret. One can only qualify this by saying that they are blinkered by their own interests, and that there is no possibility of their changing. Their own way of life and their own circle are all that matters; they are snobbery personified, not even knowing that the lower orders exist. It is important to remember that Margaret comes in part from this background and that it is a conditioning influence in her early attitudes to Milton Northern.

The other major influence is of course Helstone. It is important to reiterate that there is only one Helstone, but that if we took it as seen through Margaret's idealizing eyes and then through Mrs Hale's hypochondriacal ones, it would be two different places. Mrs Gaskell uses Helstone structurally as well, the contrast between it as a way of life and Harley Street as a way of social ambition being clearly seen when Henry Lennox comes to propose to Margaret. The symbol of the roses so loved by Margaret has been referred to elsewhere, but Mrs Gaskell's treatment is realistic and, in a compassionately ironic way, it is used as a background for Margaret's innocence and the onset of experience. Margaret befriends a poor child and an old man; later she comes to realize, in the context of Milton-Northern, what agricultural poverty is, and that Higgins should not be driven down that unending road. The return to Helstone was obviously very important from Margaret's point of view (and from the standpoint of Mrs Gaskell's aesthetic structure). It is now real still but made symbolic of mood, the death mood of the 'fatal year', as Margaret fittingly calls it. But we remember, through Mrs Gaskell's art, that it has always been symbolic of this kind of mood anyway, with the death-in-life existence of a Mrs Hale oppressed by the trees and the spiritual life-in-death existence of a Mr Hale brooding about giving up the ministry. Again the principle of contrast is employed to good effect. If masters and men can quarrel over capital and labour, then neighbours can fight over domestic cats. Human nature is the same everywhere. This is precisely what is reflected in Mrs Gaskell's deliberate use of different settings.

The third and most important setting is Milton-Northern. It is both evocative (of industry, of smoke, of throbbing, jostling life and strife) and educative, for Margaret and for its manufacturer (Thornton) and the representative of its men (Higgins). Mrs Gaskell employs the background of the industrial city to telling effect by concentrating in a broad sense on exteriors: the roads, for instance, and particularly the description of Marlborough Mills and its contiguous house. But she also concentrates on the interiors in Milton as a contrast to the pseudo-luxury of interior Harley Street; the house where Margaret and her parents live and the totally different Thornton dwelling. The interiors in these settings become symbolic of alternative ways of life or, in the case of the Higgins and Boucher homes, ways of degrading subsistence. The mill riot scene, and Bessy's account of the carding-room, provide the realism of social comment, human ambition and suffering. The writing about settings is atmospheric. What is important is that ten years after Disraeli had drawn attention to the two nations in England in *Sybil* (its title-page reads 'Or, The Two Nations') Mrs Gaskell is reiterating the problems and divisions in human and social – and one is tempted to say moral – terms. The 'human right' is the somewhat naive solution, or movement towards a solution, which Mrs Gaskell puts forward as the settings are absorbed by Margaret, for there is little doubt that she is her author's spokeswoman. Milton-Northern bestrides the novel, and Mrs Gaskell's message is as potent and certainly as relevant today as it was in her own time. It is not only our politicians and our media that tell us today of the divisions existing then, and which still exist now. It is the undeniable existence of the facts of difference. By using her settings to illustrate her themes, Mrs Gaskell is showing a cunning awareness that is a tribute to her stature as a writer and a social observer. When we go back to Harley Street in the end with Margaret we have travelled through experience; but life will never be the same again.

Style (with some references to Themes)

Mrs Gaskell has for the most part a clear narrative style. Separate headings are not given in this section, since her natural flow is often a combination of the various stylistic effects she employs. Mrs Gaskell never wrote plays, possibly because her background, her religion, her experience, did not draw her to the theatre. But she is the mistress of good, succinct and sometimes loaded *dialogue*. I suggest that a close look at the dialogue between Thornton and Margaret, or between Henry Lennox and Margaret both before and after the proposal scene, shows just how strongly Mrs Gaskell individualizes her characters through their spoken words. There are some high points of exchange too involving Mrs Thornton and Margaret and, most tellingly, between Mrs Thornton and her son.

Edith's indolence is perfectly conveyed through her words. Even in the first chapter, the overheard conversation shows how accurately Mrs Gaskell catches the superficial tone and the note of complaint; Mrs Shaw's remarks about the General do not make her a caricature, they make her recognizable to us because we know people like her. The richly aggressive speech of Dixon helps to define her individuality, and the querulous Mrs Hale, the diffident and inadequate Mr Hale, the wit (and wisdom) of Mr Bell rarely strike a false note. Where one can be less happy about Mrs Gaskell's achievement is in her handling of *dialect*, and this is strange. Mrs Gaskell normally has a good ear, and Mr Gaskell appended some notes to the dialect of *Mary Barton*. But there are times when Nicholas's 'hoo' seems strained, and times too when there is a curious mix of dialogue in received standard English and dialect. This is not, of course, to criticize Mrs Gaskell's use of dialect words, many of which, as in a Hardy novel, give the text a richness of particularity that would otherwise be missing. But she is perhaps trying too hard through dialect speech to convey the inflexions she had heard so often when visiting the poor. The dialect speech is not obtrusive, and does not spoil the effect, but jars every now and then on the ear.

Mrs Gaskell is a fine *descriptive* writer, and this is particularly evident in the Helstone chapter early on, when she has detailed natural descriptions, sometimes with poetic observation and emphases. She is equally good at bringing alive an individual, and there are three notable set-pieces of description, which bring out the physical lineaments of Margaret, Thornton and his mother. With Margaret she is particularly successful, since she manages to convey her sexual attraction through certain words (her 'flexile' neck, for instance) and also through movement. Margaret is 'lithe', but her movement in the streets and, for instance, when she goes with Frederick to the station, compel admiration from passers-by. We are always aware of Margaret as a presence, and the same quality applies to most of the other characters. But if Mrs Gaskell is a telling creator of character in its physical aspects, she is also, as we have seen from the section on Settings, a very good observer and recorder of the details of interiors, the best example of this being the Thornton house (and one particular room) before Margaret and Mr Hale pay their visit. Mrs Gaskell has a superb sense of place and the atmosphere of place, and this is one of her greatest assets.

If outward description is impressive in *North and South*, it would be true to say that it is matched by *inward analysis* of the consciousness that gives her characters their psychological truth. The main burden here is borne by Margaret, and complements the burdens she bears throughout the action of the novel. The 'stream of consciousness', which is so marked a part of twentieth-century writing, is present in nineteenth-century fiction too. Margaret, in reaction to her father's disturbing decision, or after overhearing her name coupled with Thornton's when she has tried to protect him, is all consciousness. Thornton, in reaction to Margaret's rejection of him, is frustrated consciousness; his mother is angry and apprehensive consciousness when she fears that she will lose her son to Margaret. These three merit close attention and exposure. Mrs Gaskell is more reticent in her treatment of Mr and Mrs Hale, where more of the inward constituents might have revealed more of the incompatibility. Even here there is method in her measure, for neither character must usurp the central functional realism of Margaret. There is little attempt to explore the consciousness of superficial characters like Edith and Mrs Shaw, or of characters like Dixon, Higgins and Bessy. Their spoken words say all that needs to be said.

Mrs Gaskell's main stylistic device, seen in various modes, is that of *irony*, in sophisticated sarcasm about sophisticated people, and with a due weight of compassion in her presentation of suffering. Harley Street calls forth the kind of Gaskellian irony that distinguishes the portrait of Mrs Kirkpatrick in *Wives and Daughters*. And when

Margaret goes back to Harley Street after her bereavements, things are no better:

The elements of the dinner-parties which Mrs Lennox gave, were these; her friends contributed the beauty, Captain Lennox the easy knowledge of the subjects of the day; and Mr Henry Lennox and the sprinkling of rising men who were received as his friends, brought the wit, the cleverness, the keen and extensive knowledge of which they knew well enough how to avail themselves without seeming pedantic, or burdening the rapid flow of conversation. (Chapter 48)

This irony embraces the reminiscences of Mrs Shaw about the age difference between herself and the General, and Edith's apparently regarding keeping a piano in tune as one of the most important aspects of married life.

Mrs Gaskell enjoys herself at the expense of Henry Lennox, who employs his own irony after his rejection. But, best of all, Mrs Gaskell's irony embraces Margaret herself, but with compassion because Margaret, despite being commendable in almost every way, never passes into complacency (nor is her creator complacent about her) and certainly she is never outside the orbit of our sympathetic concern. Yet Margaret, as Bessy said she would, sins. She tells the saving lie, and the author's irony suggests that this good and thoroughly Christian girl has done so for the right reason. Yet when we know that Frederick has got clean away, and that Thornton has assisted in a cover-up of Margaret (ironic too) Margaret's pride will not let her clear it up with Thornton. Moreover, she loves him, yet knows it not. There is little humour in Margaret's life, but there is a kind of amused irony, always tolerant, in the way she is viewed by her creator. Arguably, the whole of the Helstone return visit is ironic, since all that Margaret thought turns out to be misplaced. The author's irony ultimately helps to place Margaret where she can do the most good. But there is a cunning might-have-been which is part of the ironic mode: would Margaret and Thornton ever have come together if she had not become an heiress?

These are the main stylistic devices in *North and South*, and we do not intend to look at any others in close detail. There is the continued use of *contrast*, which underlines the title of the novel, which itself stresses an essential and important *Theme*. The themes of *conflict* are fully explored, masters and men being contrasted. There is also a considered use of *retrospect*, mainly to fill in either facets of Margaret's childhood or, for instance, the details of the mutiny that changed the

Hales' lives. The author's use of her own voice, so common in nineteenth-century fiction and so pronounced in the advocacy of reconciliation in *Mary Barton*, is here virtually in abeyance. Mrs Gaskell does use *imagery*, but never with a consistent and reiterative purpose as, for example, George Eliot does. She does use *symbols* on occasions, and there are references, in one or two chapter commentaries, to the importance of the Helstone roses as romantic and ironic comment on Margaret.

Mrs Gaskell can be *melodramatic*, as with the return of Frederick or the visit of the police inspector to question Margaret; she can be *impassioned*, as in Thornton's words of love over the senseless Margaret. She can use the common device of *the letter*, as when Edith writes to Margaret one which contrasts so poignantly with Margaret's own surroundings – a breath of the warm south in Margaret's bleak north. Mrs Gaskell commands variety, her style is supple and pervaded with the needs and essence of a situation. She can be *bathetic*, as when Mrs Thornton cries out for her baby son who is the grown-up Frederick, but these are rare descents. The verve of her narrative depends on the interaction of the outward and the inward, and she is adept at balancing these in the onward revelations that constitute the fictional experience.

General questions

1 Write an essay defending Mrs Gaskell's choice of *Margaret Hale* for the title of her novel.

Guideline Notes

    (a) Introductory paragraph – the main concerns of the novel in the broad sense, but with an emphasis on the fact that virtually all the action is seen through Margaret's eyes.

    (b) Our first meeting with Margaret – impressions – the set-up in Harley Street – Margaret's reminiscences of her first stay there – the role she has of poor but valued relation.

    (c) Helstone – Margaret and family affairs – Margaret and Lennox – Margaret and organization of the move. Focus on her being firm and consistent.

    (d) Early responses to Milton – to Thornton – meeting with Higgins and Bessy – worry over mother – over Frederick – the riot at the Mill.

    (e) Margaret and the letter to Frederick – her awareness of Thornton – mother's death – the saving lie – death of father – Mr Bell – Harley Street – return to Helstone. Final Harley street scene with Thornton.

    (f) Conclusion – social issues very important to Mrs Gaskell, but Margaret at centre of everything.

2 Write an essay bringing out fully Mrs Gaskell's use of contrast in *North and South*.

3 Compare and contrast the characters of Henry Lennox and John Thornton. In what ways do they represent the differences between the south and the north?

4 'In dealing with the industrial scene Mrs Gaskell is completely naive.' Discuss.

5 Write a character study of *one* of the following: (a) Nicholas Higgins; (b) Mr Hale; (c) Mr Bell; (d) Edith.

6 With particular reference to one or more scenes, indicate Mrs Gaskell's ability to create a graphic and exciting atmosphere.

7 What are the main divisions between masters and men in *North and South*? You should refer closely to the text in your answer.

8 Compare and contrast Mrs Hale and Mrs Thornton.

9 Why is the return to Helstone an essential part of the structure of *North and South*? You should quote from the relevant chapter in your answer, or refer closely to it.

10 When, and where, is Mrs Gaskell guilty of writing melodramatically? Refer closely to the text.

11 Account for the friction between Thornton and Margaret. In what ways is each to blame for this?

12 Write an essay on the main aspects of Mrs Gaskell's style in *North and South*.

13 In what ways does Mrs Gaskell employ irony in *North and South*?

14 'Although she is the heroine, she is not very likeable.' How far would you agree with this assessment of Margaret?

15 Indicate the part played by Bessy Higgins in the novel. Do you think that she is an important influence on Margaret?

16 'Some of her minor characters are poorly drawn.' How far do you think that this is true of *North and South*?

17 'The best drawn character in the novel.' Would you agree with this evaluation of Dixon?

Further reading

Texts

North and South, (ed. Dorothy Collin) Penguin English Library, 1970.
North and South, (ed. Angus Easson) World's Classics, OUP, 1982.

Biography and criticism

Elizabeth Gaskell: A Portrait in Letters (ed. J. A. V. Chapple and J. G. Sharps) Manchester University Press, 1980.

Elizabeth Gaskell: by Winifred Gerin, OUP, 1980.

Mrs Gaskell: Novelist and Biographer: by Arthur Pollard, Manchester University Press, 1965.

Elizabeth Gaskell: by Angus Easson, OUP, 1976.

Brodie's Notes

D. H. Lawrence	The Rainbow
D. H. Lawrence	Sons and Lovers
D. H. Lawrence	Women in Love
Harper Lee	To Kill a Mockingbird
Laurie Lee	Cider with Rosie
Christopher Marlowe	Dr Faustus
Arthur Miller	The Crucible
Arthur Miller	Death of a Salesman
John Milton	Paradise Lost
Robert C. O'Brien	Z for Zachariah
Sean O'Casey	Juno and the Paycock
George Orwell	Animal Farm
George Orwell	1984
J. B. Priestley	An Inspector Calls
J. D. Salinger	The Catcher in the Rye
William Shakespeare	Antony and Cleopatra
William Shakespeare	As You Like It
William Shakespeare	Hamlet
William Shakespeare	Henry IV Part I
William Shakespeare	Julius Caesar
William Shakespeare	King Lear
William Shakespeare	Macbeth
William Shakespeare	Measure for Measure
William Shakespeare	The Merchant of Venice
William Shakespeare	A Midsummer Night's Dream
William Shakespeare	Much Ado about Nothing
William Shakespeare	Othello
William Shakespeare	Richard II
William Shakespeare	Romeo and Juliet
William Shakespeare	The Tempest
William Shakespeare	Twelfth Night
George Bernard Shaw	Pygmalion
Alan Sillitoe	Selected Fiction
John Steinbeck	Of Mice and Men and The Pearl
Jonathan Swift	Gulliver's Travels
Dylan Thomas	Under Milk Wood
Alice Walker	The Color Purple
W. B. Yeats	Selected Poetry

ENGLISH COURSEWORK BOOKS

Terri Apter	Women and Society
Kevin Dowling	Drama and Poetry
Philip Gooden	Conflict
Philip Gooden	Science Fiction
Margaret K. Gray	Modern Drama
Graham Handley	Modern Poetry
Graham Handley	Prose
Graham Handley	Childhood and Adolescence
R. J. Sims	The Short Story